Money

Money

How to Make the Most of What You've Got

William J. Lynott

Authors Choice Press
San Jose New York Lincoln Shanghai

Money
How to Make the Most of What You've Got

Authors Choice Press
an imprint of iUniverse.com, Inc.

For information address:
iUniverse.com, Inc.
620 North 48th Street, Suite 201
Lincoln, NE 68504-3467
www.iuniverse.com

ISBN: 0-595-13524-2

Printed in the United States of America

To Betty Lou who put me on the right track, in more ways than one.

Contents

List of Tables

Preface

Money is a singular thing. It ranks with love as man's greatest source of joy. And with death as his greatest source of anxiety. Over all history it has oppressed nearly all people in one of two ways: either it has been abundant and very unreliable, or reliable and very scarce.

—John Kenneth Galbraith, U.S. Economist (b.1908)

Money: It's a fundamental part of our lives from the first day mommy tucks lunch money into our back packs until we finally shuffle off this mortal coil.

How much of the stuff we manage to earn, how much of it we save, what we do with it—these things, perhaps more than any other, determine what niche we are destined to occupy in the complex hierarchy of today's society.

Money and our ability to manage it determines how well we live, how well we are able to care for our families, how well we sleep at night and, yes, how well we will enjoy our golden years. So, how come, after dealing with the stuff every day of our lives since early childhood, so many of us are total klutzes in the way we handle it?

It would take someone with fancier credentials than mine to answer that poser. Is there anyone out there with a psychology/sociology/biology/economics degree?

I suspect not. That's why I suggest that we pass up the temptation to engage in theoretical analysis of this American phenomenon. Let's take a more practical approach.

We'll concentrate on the simple steps that you can take to ensure that you'll never become a target for the slings and arrows that Dame Fortune likes to direct at those of us foolish enough to neglect our fiscal education.

Later in these pages you're going to learn the four most important words in the world of personal finance. This four-word phrase is so important that it may well be worth a million or more dollars to you. And yet, an astonishing number of people have never heard it...or failed to understand it if they did hear it. Make no mistake, when it comes to money, what you don't know can, and probably will, hurt you.

But don't worry. I'm not going to ask you to deal with scholarly definitions of the M1 money supply or esoteric systems for identifying undervalued stocks—investments sure to make you an overnight millionaire. A visit to your local bookstore will quickly reveal that those topics have already been covered in exhaustive, if not exhausting, detail. Instead, this book will help guide you through the fiscal maze that has prevented millions of Americans from enjoying maximum benefit from whatever level of earning power they have achieved, all because they never bothered to learn the basics.

***

If there was a single moment that provided the genesis for this effort, it was the time my grandson asked me for some tips on handling money. Recently graduated from high school, he was preparing to leave for college.

"How does a checking account work?" he asked, "and what, exactly, is a CD?"

Those questions came as something of a shock to me. How could a student having just completed 12 years of successful navigation through primary and secondary schools in a much-honored school system not know how a checking account works? Could it be that he was the only student in his graduating class who failed to absorb such financial rudiments? Or could it be that 12 years of schooling, which is all that many Americans ever get, did not include even a brief introduction to the world of personal finance?

School administrators provided the answers. Yes, courses in personal finance are part of our local high school curriculum…but they are **elective** courses. Students received no such instructions unless they had enough foresight to choose them as electives.

And how many students are likely to display that sort of forethought? Not many, according to a 1999 survey by the American Savings Education Council in Washington, D.C. Their study found that most students, ages 16 to 22, had never taken a high school or college course in personal finance.

"Most high school seniors graduate as financial illiterates," says Dara Duguay, executive director of JumpStart, a coalition of 86 companies, government agencies and nonprofit organizations.

A little reminiscing about my own foresight, or lack of same, at age 15 or 16 left little doubt about how I might have handled such an important responsibility. Fortunately for me, we weren't called on to exercise financial vision during my public school years. As early as junior high school, I clearly remember being instructed in the basics of such things as balancing a checkbook and the power of compound interest—whether I liked it or not.

Of course, fifty years ago, the world was a far simpler place. There was less to learn and fewer pitfalls waiting to ensnare the unwary. "A penny saved is a penny earned" was pretty much all we had to know in those days.

It's far different today. Making the most of your resources in today's hardscrabble financial arena is a much more demanding and potentially rewarding task.

So, surely those students who are fortunate enough to gain entrance into the Halls of Academe are at long last receiving a thorough grounding in the art of handling their personal finances

Apparently not. One doesn't have to look very hard to find physicians, lawyers and other much-lettered academics and scientists who are hopelessly inept at dealing with their personal financial affairs.

While an extended formal education is still the best gateway to a better-than-average income, it is by no means a guarantee that you will gain optimum benefit from your earning power.

A professional acquaintance of mine, I'll call him Mark, is a good illustration of this curious phenomenon. Mark's annual income is well into six figures and has been for some years. He's 40 years old and still hasn't saved a penny. He and his wife live an extravagant life style that takes every cent he earns. Mark himself admits that he just doesn't know where his money goes.

He'd better find out soon. With three children approaching college age, Mark is in for a rude awakening. When it comes to making the most of your good fortune, there are some things that even the best courses in the best schools won't teach you.

***

Clearly, your ability to **earn** money will be the primary indicator of how far up the economic ladder you will climb. But it is not necessarily an indication of how well you will live. I will always remember my late mother-in-law whose husband never earned more than a modest salary. Through an instinctive understanding of the basic rules of money management, she was able to parlay their limited income into a lifestyle that belied their relatively low perch on the economic ladder. She was living proof of the effectiveness of the principles outlined in this book, long before I knew they existed.

The world abounds with people like Mark. People who earn a great deal of money but never seem to have a dime to spare. This book cannot help you to become one of the former, but I believe it can help to keep you from becoming one of the latter.

CHAPTER ONE

Money—How It All Started

The universal regard for money is the one hopeful fact in our civilisation. Money is the most important thing in the world. It represents health, strength, honour, generosity and beauty.... Not the least of its virtues is that it destroys base people as certainly as it fortifies and dignifies noble people.

—George Bernard Shaw (1856–1950)

No one knows the exact moment when the first person said (or grunted), "You have something I want and I have something you want, so let's swap."

While history does not afford us that knowledge, we do know that "swapping" or bartering as a way of exchanging goods and services has been around for a long time. It came into existence at least a few millenia before someone got the idea of using "money" as an easier way to oil the wheels of commerce.

It is probably safe for us to assume that the earliest civilizations were already well underway when the idea of bartering emerged. Before that, back in the caveman days, if someone had something you wanted, you simply took it (provided you were stronger and/or could run faster than the person from whom you planned to take it).

Bartering served a critically important function in the earliest civilizations. When two people had items of comparable value that they wanted to swap bartering filled the bill. Still, the system suffered from some obvious shortcomings.

Suppose, for example, that I have a fat pig that I would like to swap and you would dearly love to have. However, all you have available for swapping is some extra corn. Let's suppose further that I already have lots of corn. Under those conditions, I may well tell you to get lost; I already have all the corn I need. In that stalemate, I'll be left with a surplus of pigs, and you'll have your corn, but no pigs. Pure frustration. The wheels of commerce have ground to a halt.

That's the way it was in economies ruled by barter—the direct exchange of one commodity for another. In a barter economy, a person having something to trade must find someone who wants it and has something acceptable to offer in exchange. There had to be a better way.

Enter money.

The idea behind the evolution of money was simple enough: Let's come up with a medium of exchange that is widely accepted in payment for goods and services and in settlement of debts. This new medium must also serve as a standard of value for measuring the relative worth of different goods and services. That way, if I want your fat pig, I can simply "buy" it, provided I have accumulated enough of this new medium of exchange to cover the pig's fair market value.

Finally, as money evolved, it was no longer necessary to search around for someone who had exactly what you needed and who wanted what you had to offer in trade. Money was of universal value. It could be used by anyone to buy anything.

Some scholars maintain that the clumsy and inadequate nature of bartering was not the primary factor behind the evolution of money. Such "non-economic" factors as customs or laws requiring some form of payment in compensation for crimes, is one example they cite. Then there was the custom requiring payment to the father of a bride to compensate for the loss of her services.

Whether these and other customs were economic or non-economic factors are weighty matters best left to the scholars to debate. For our purposes, we'll look at the evolution of money simply as a natural solution to the limitations of bartering.

***

Of course, the first forms of money bore little resemblance to the money we take for granted today. Money did not originate at one specific place or time. It evolved gradually and simultaneously in many parts of the world.

At different times and different places, commodities used as money included such things as beads, sea shells, eggs, stones, feathers, gold, silver, ivory, jade, leather, nails, salt, cattle, elephant tusks, furs, wampum, whales' teeth, even pigs. Almost anything regarded as valuable in a given society could be, and was, used as a medium of exchange.

In fact, primitive forms of money are still being used in some societies in the Third World and even in North America. Some items originally used as forms of bodily ornamentation gradually came into use as money. Polished shell beads, traditionally used as a medium of exchange by Native American tribes, are a good example. Originally worn as decoration and insignia of rank, the beads were strung on hemp strings or woven into belts. Both unstrung beads and finished belts were used in trade. Wampum belts were also used to formalize transactions between tribes. A communication from one tribe or council to another became official with the delivery of a belt woven into a pattern representing the message or treaty that it represented.

In *A History of Money*, author Glyn Davies provides this universally accepted definition: "Money is anything that is widely used for making payments and accounting for debts and credits."

Money has also been described as a standard of value for measuring the relative worth of goods and services offered in the marketplace. Thus, the number of units of money required to buy a given commodity can be said to be the "price" of that commodity. These two simple definitions of money provide everything we need in order to understand the principles of personal financial management outlined in this book.

While various forms of early money solved many problems associated with the cumbersome bartering system, they introduced a few problems of their own. People fortunate enough to accumulate a bit of wealth had to think about such things as where to store their "money." You can't hide 1,000 pigs (or even one pig) under your mattress. And your discretion (as well as your safety) would be called into question if you stacked a few dozen gold bars in your cave. Then there was the question of durability to be considered. A dozen eggs may have been very valuable in some societies, but their shelf life imposed an obvious limitation.

Problems of this sort were solved neatly with the coming of coinage, the first examples of what we might call modern money. It isn't possible for us to say with certainty where and when coins first came into use as a standard medium of exchange. However, we do know that they've been around since long before the time of Christ.

Among the earliest metallic "coins" were so-called cowries made of bronze or copper in ancient China. The ancient Greeks used iron nails as coins. The Britons were minting true coins long before they were conquered by the Romans.

The biggest trouble with these early coins was that they were too easy to counterfeit. Made of base metal with little or no intrinsic value, they were clearly inadequate for the task of supporting increasingly complex economies.

The first small round stampings of precious metal designed to make counterfeiting more difficult are attributed to the Lydians of Asia Minor. As the Lydians gained experience, their coins gradually improved in both consistency and quality. Soon, the idea of precious metal coins spread from Lydia to mainland Greece and Persia. From there the idea of issuing coinage as money gradually became everybody's ball game.

In time, all of the major ancient societies developed their own versions of coinage; the Babylonians had their shekels, the Greeks had their drachmas, the Macedonians had their tetradrachmas, the Bohemians had their talers, to name a few.

One reason for the rapid spread of coins as money was the obvious convenience of not having to weigh them (or feed them, for that matter). Counting was obviously more convenient, and more fun, than weighing or feeding.

By the Middle Ages, the royal mints were churning out coins that were assigned significantly higher values than the intrinsic value of their metallic content. Thus, royal families were able to pocket the difference as a nice profit on their own coins of the realm. This neat little trick was enhanced by the recall of all coins every few years so that the king might mint a new batch, thus enhancing his personal larder even further.

***

While coins were an obvious improvement over rocks and seashells, they were still cumbersome in large quantities. Carrying enough money in a pants pocket for a night on the town could risk an embarrassing encounter with gravity. This problem, as well as a few others, was solved with the introduction of paper money. By making one slip of paper equal to the value of many coins, a government could greatly simplify the handling of money. That, in turn, made it easier for everyone to do business. And, of course, pants pockets lasted a lot longer.

As we have seen thus far, money comes in many varieties. The most important of these have come to be called commodity money, credit money, and fiat money.

The value of commodity money is roughly equal to the value of the material contained in it. Early coins of gold, silver, or copper are examples of commodity money. The gold coins minted and circulated in the United States before 1933 were a modern example of commodity money.

Credit money is paper money backed by promises by the issuer, which can be a government or a bank, to pay an equivalent value in the standard monetary metal.

Paper money, the value of which is fixed solely by government edict that cannot be exchanged for any other type of money, is known as fiat money.

For the most part, both fiat and credit forms of money are made acceptable only through a government decree that all creditors must accept the official money in settlement of any and all debts. Thus, the money is officially decreed to be legal tender. Not only are today's American paper notes an example of fiat money, our coins are as well, since their metal content is worth less than the official declared value of the coins. Today, the monetary systems of most other countries of the world are fiat systems as well.

Now that you know the difference between commodity money, credit money and fiat money, you can forget all about it. For our purposes here, money is money. The only type of money that you're likely to be dealing with is good old U.S. dollars, and I think you already know what they are.

***

Since America was a Johnny-come-lately in the evolution of money, we didn't have to endure the trials and tribulations of its early development. Although bartering was practiced to a limited degree in early America (and still is under some circumstances), the modern concept of money was pretty much in place by the time the Pilgrims first sloshed their way onto Plymouth Rock.

Sophisticated coins of almost every European country were put to use in the American colonies right from the beginning. Early in the evolution of modern money, the Spanish dollar was the most prominent. Still, some remnants of ancient coinage could have been found if one looked hard enough. Some hardy American colonists used commodities such as bullets, tobacco, and animal skins as mediums of exchange.

The first truly national American currency consisted of paper notes issued by the Continental Congress in 1775 to finance the American Revolution. These notes were originally declared redeemable in gold or silver coins. The trouble was that more notes were printed than could be redeemed by the revolutionary government's scant supply of precious metal coins. As a result, shortly after the successful end of that war, the notes became nearly worthless.

In 1792, the foundling United States passed the first coinage act. The new legislation adopted a bimetallic standard, the terms of which called for the first minting of American coins in both gold and silver. The new gold dollar contained exactly 24 and 3/4 grains of pure gold. Silver dollars contained exactly 15 times that weight of silver, establishing gold as worth 15 times the same quantity of silver.

American money had almost always been backed by commodities, but that changed during the Civil War of 1861 to 1865. The governments of both the Union and the Confederacy found it necessary to finance their needs through the issuance of fiat money. Thus, the notes issued by the Confederate treasury and the Southern states became worthless after the war. The U.S. notes (called greenbacks then) and other paper money issued by the federal government depreciated rapidly, but retained some value.

In 1863 the National Banking Act authorized the establishment of national banks that could issue bank notes backed by government bonds.

In the late 1800s there was a movement to establish silver as the standard of currency, but in 1900 the Gold Standard Act affirmed the gold dollar as the standard unit of monetary value in the United States.

The next major change in our monetary system was introduced by the Federal Reserve Act of 1913. This landmark legislation created the Federal Reserve System, which, in turn, resulted in the issuance of the first Federal Reserve notes. The new currency was immediately declared the standard currency for this country.

The Great Depression and the epidemic of bank failures in the early 1930s led to further reforms in the nation's monetary structure. One of the most important of these changes was the ending of the gold standard. The country later returned to a modified gold standard with a devalued dollar. Silver was also coined and added to the monetary base.

An historic meeting on international finance, known as the Bretton Woods Conference, took place during World War II. The result, in 1944, was a new international monetary system in which the U.S. dollar played the key role. It became, in effect, the standard for the world's currency when all members of the International Monetary Fund (IMF) defined the value of their own currencies relative to the dollar. As part of this financial coalition, the United States agreed to convert all dollars held by foreign governments into gold on demand.

This new arrangement seemed to work quite smoothly until the quantity of dollars held by foreign governments began to exceed U.S. gold holdings by huge amounts. It was clear by then to everyone, even the most sanguine believers in the gold standard, that the system was beginning to falter. In 1971, in recognition of the problem, the United States decided to suspend gold payments of U.S. dollars.

Since the end of the gold standard, the United States has had a fully managed currency system, one with no precious metal standard of any kind. Thus, in a relatively short time, we have gone from a wholly metallic system, when coins with intrinsic value were the primary money in circulation, to a totally managed system, in which most of the fiat money in circulation consists of entries in the books and computers of institutions called banks.

Where did banks come from? Why do we need them? Turn the page and we'll take a hard look at those solemn institutions and how they can, and do, affect your life.

CHAPTER TWO

Banks—A (very) Short History

Ready money is Aladdin's lamp.
—Lord Byron (1788–1824)

Bankers (moneychangers) have been around as long as money itself. Even before the advent of coinage, bankers were poised to extract their pound of flesh…er, grain.

Once money became an accepted medium of exchange, people who were lucky enough to accumulate a little of the stuff needed a place to stash their cash. In addition, some people, like many of us today, needed to borrow money.

There are conflicting opinions as to what country deserves the credit (or blame) for giving birth to the first bankers. Some historians say the idea of banking originated in ancient Mesopotamia. In that country, royal palaces and temples were offered as secure storage places for grain and other valuable commodities. Citizens making such deposits were given official receipts. Soon, those receipts were being used for transfers not only back to the original depositors, but also to third parties. You'll remember from the previous chapter how activity of that sort might well be considered the use of what is called commodity money.

Over time, private organizations in Mesopotamia began to get involved in these transactions. Soon thereafter, came Mesopotamian laws regulating these new institutions. Thus, in the eyes of some, banking was born.

However, around that same time, similar goings on were taking place in Egypt as well. In that country, the storage of grain harvests in royal warehouses also resulted in the issuance of receipts. Those receipts, too, gradually came into use for payment of debts and other financial transactions.

The earliest known banking records indicate that another ancient country, Babylon, had a highly developed banking system as early as 2000 BC It was known as the Igibi Bank of Babylon and it may have been the world's first private banking system. Like the banks of today, the Igibi bank paid interest on deposits and lent money to needy souls, provided they were able to meet the bank's qualifications.

As you might imagine, the early Romans weren't any slouches in the financial arena. They had their own versions of banking. In ancient Rome, all banking operations were private enterprises carefully regulated by law, at least until the Emperor Augustus decided to take over the banking business himself.

After the fall of the Roman Empire, Augustus faded into memory. Not long after that, the Romans outlawed banking altogether, calling it an illegal and harmful practice.

By the third century, AD, banking conducted by private individuals was allowed once again. The new bankers organized institutions that came to be known as "poverty banks." These lasted until the 13th century when banking was monopolized again—this time by the churches.

By the fourteenth century, when profitable ocean trade routes were gradually being developed, privately owned banks were again allowed to operate. With the coming of international shipments of valuable commodities such as spices, silk, and gold, which had to be financed by wealthy individuals and organizations, banking rapidly became big business.

***

Except for dedicated occupants of the Halls of Academe, none of this untidy business really matters much. What matters is that banks have been with us for a very long time and are likely to be with us until the end. And the more you know about how they work, the more effectively you can deal with them.

The first "banking" operations involved only commodities. This included precious metals, all of which had to be weighed to determine their value. While there were some exceptions, almost all of the very early forms of "money" were based on weight.

The original meaning of the Greek word *drachma* was a "hand full of grain"—not very precise, but easily understood by peasant and royalty alike. Many financial terms in use today such as "spend" and "expenditure" have their roots in the Latin word, *expendere,* which means "to weigh." The monetary unit, talent, from the Biblical *Parable of the Talents*, was a Greek unit of weight amounting to about 60 of today's pounds.

Gradually, as coins came into general use, the idea of weighing gave way to counting as the accepted method for quantifying money. Counting, after all, was quicker and much more convenient than weighing, and certainly more precise, provided that one had received at least a smidgen of instruction in arithmetic. Through it all, the bankers were there, providing an admittedly valuable service for the common man…but always at a cost.

Today's banks, while they bear many similarities to their progenitors, are very different animals. They operate in an entirely different, far more sophisticated, financial arena. More important, they touch the life of every person in our society, including you. While the history of banking in ancient times is often spotty and imprecise, we know exactly how banking evolved in America. You don't have to know a great deal about the history of our banks to be a successful money manager, but, hey, it won't hurt.

***

The first Bank of the United States was chartered by the Congress of the United States in 1791. Twenty years later, it was dissolved when the second Bank of the United States came into existence. It, too, lasted only about 20 years, from 1816 to 1836. These first banks were created basically to provide currency to colonists who needed a uniform means of exchange. The banks issued notes for money deposited and made loans.

After the closing of the second Bank of the United States, most of the paper currency in circulation in the country consisted of notes issued by banks chartered by individual states. The currencies from these banks circulated mostly within the limited areas served by the individual banks.

Gradually, a series of laws evolved designed to stabilize the country's banking industry and maintain the confidence of the general public. Sometimes, these legislative acts served their purpose well, sometimes not. At various times in America's early history, public confidence in banks faltered, occasionally resulting in runs on the banks. A run occurs when large numbers of depositors descend on a bank all at once demanding all of their money. Needless to say, that can spell disaster for a bank or, if the problem is widespread, for an entire banking system. Among the more important of the banking laws designed to strengthen our banking system over the years were:

(1863) The National Banking Act. This new law permitted national bank charters and operations for the first time. They were to be governed under rules established by the U.S. government, which was required to issue paper currency and back it up with the full faith and credit of the federal government. This law was passed at a time when public confidence in the banking system was at a low ebb. The new legislation was intended to restore the public's confidence in banks and money in general.

(1913) The Federal Reserve Act was passed. This new legislation created a system of 12 regional government banks and a board of governors. The purpose of the new system was to coordinate the efforts of other banks, stabilize the flow of currency, and avoid runs on any given bank. It also allowed banks to borrow from the Federal Reserve to cover excessive and sudden withdrawals that might occur during a financial panic.

In today's world, the Federal Reserve serves several important functions, all designed to stabilize our economy and foster a sound banking system. Entire books can be written on the structure and operation of the "Fed," but you don't need to concern yourself with the details unless you're a glutton for punishment.

You may have read or heard about organizations and individuals dedicated to the proposition that the Fed is illegal, unconstitutional, immoral and ineffective. Such talk is pure nonsense.

While the system is far from perfect, it has helped to foster the most stable and prosperous economy of any developed country in the world. We'd all better get used to it because it's going to be around for a long time.

In total, the 12 Federal Reserve Banks process more than one-third of all checks written in the United States. That amounts to more than $12 trillion annually. More important, the total dollar volume moving through the Federal reserve's system is nearing $200 trillion. That's many times America's gross national product.

(1933) The Federal Deposit Insurance Corporation (FDIC) was a child of the Great Depression. It was born at a time when the public's confidence in the banking system was arguably at its lowest point in America's history. The act provided federally funded insurance of at least $5,000 for each individual's account, even if the bank that held the account failed. This amount has been increased over the years. Today, individual accounts in member banks are automatically insured at no charge up to a maximum of $100,000.

***

Before you deposit any money in any bank, make sure it is a member of the FDIC. While almost all of today's banks are FDIC members, there are still a few that are not. Most member banks display the FDIC logo prominently on their windows and in their literature. A similar organization, The Federal Savings & Loan Insurance Corporation (FSLIC), offers the same insurance protection to depositors in member savings & loan associations.

(1980) The Depository Institutions Deregulation and Monetary Control Act eliminated a law known as Regulation Q. This questionable law had established legal limits on the interest rates that banks and other institutions were allowed to pay on time deposits and savings accounts.

With the passing of the new law, banks were free to compete with each other on the basis of how much interest they were willing to pay in order to attract depositors. This competition is in full swing today. As you will see later, using this competition to your advantage is an important element in good money management strategy.

Enough of that dry history. Let's get down to the nitty gritty of banking today and what you need to know to gain the advantage in this arranged marriage between you and the banks.

***

What is a Bank, anyway?

Think the answer to that question is easy? Well hold on. Actually, the term "bank" is widely used to describe a number of different kinds of businesses. What you think of as your local "bank" may be a commercial bank, a savings and loan association, a savings bank, or a credit union. While there are many similarities in these institutions, they are not the same. We'll discuss some of those differences later.

In general, when most people use the term bank, they are referring to what is called a commercial bank. This is the most common form of bank in the United States. The odds are that you have at least one account in a commercial bank.

A commercial bank is generally defined as a privately owned institution that accepts demand deposits and makes loans to businesses.

What is a demand deposit? That's simply money that you and other bank customers leave in an institution with the understanding that you can get it back any time you want it—on demand.

As far as loans are concerned, we all know what they are. Don't we? Of course, banks provide other services in addition to loans, many of which have become essential to our modern economy.

How important are banks to our economic system? One estimate says that, at any one time, America's banks hold 40% of all of this country's assets. One person who seemingly had an instinctive understanding of this interesting situation was notorious bank robber, Willie Sutton. When asked by a newspaper reporter why he robbed banks, Sutton replied simply, "Because that's where the money is."

Most people and businesses now pay their bills with bank checking accounts. Banks also provide loans to individual consumers as well as businesses. Banks are, in fact, the major source of consumer loans used to buy cars, finance mortgages for homes, and pay for educations.

Banks are often described as the engines of our economy. One reason is the assortment of functions they provide like those described above. But there is yet another reason why banks are so important. It is through banks that our government's monetary policy is put into practice. This is done largely through the Federal Reserve System discussed earlier.

Banks aren't allowed to lend out all the deposits they take in. If they did, they wouldn't be able to give the money back if large numbers of depositors descended on the banks at the same time demanding their money. That's why government regulations require that they keep primary and secondary reserves. Federal law sets requirements for the percentage of deposits a bank must keep on reserve, either at the local Federal Reserve Bank or in its own vault. Any money a bank has on hand after it meets its reserve requirement is its excess reserves. It is this money in excess of required reserves that is lent out to businesses and individuals.

It's obvious from all this that banks play a vital role in our economy and in the lives of individuals in our society. But don't allow yourself to think that banks are charitable institutions.

***

How Banks Make Money

Although banks are important cogs in our economic machinery, it is important for you to understand a basic fact about them. With the exception of Federal Reserve Banks and mutual banks owned by the depositors, they are privately owned, for-profit institutions. Banks are owned by stockholders who have made their investments for the sole purpose of generating a profitable return on those investments. Their stockholders expect the management of the banks to generate satisfactory profits. At the end of each year, banks pay some or all of their profits to their shareholders in the form of dividends, just as for-profit corporations do. Most banks retain some portion of their profits to add to working capital for expansion and growth.

There is certainly nothing wrong with this exercise in our capitalist economy. Still, it's important for you to disabuse yourself of any notion that banks are run by kindly philanthropists who lie awake at night thinking about new ways to save you money and pay you more interest.

Banks use the money you deposit with them to earn money in three ways:

1. They make money from what is called the "spread." The spread is simply the difference between the rate of interest banks pay for deposits you leave with them and the interest rate they charge on the loans they make to others (or even to you). Keep in mind that the less interest they pay you for your deposits, the higher the spread (profit) for them.

2. Banks earn interest on the securities they have purchased with some of the reserve money they are required to set aside.

3. Banks charge fees for services they render, such as checking accounts, the use of ATM machines, financial counseling, and servicing loans. Charges like these, many of which have historically been furnished free of charge, are now growing at what some consumer activists feel is an objectionable rate. These are the charges that you should learn to minimize or eliminate entirely. You'll learn how later.

The checking account first appeared in the mid-19th century. It was the first "extra" service provided by banks. Today, the list includes credit cards, automatic teller machines (ATM's), NOW accounts, various types of retirement accounts, home equity loans, and a growing list of enticing (and often expensive) financial services.

Over the years, banking laws have been changed to allow other financial institutions to perform some banking functions. Banks now compete with savings and loans, savings banks, credit unions, financing companies, investment banks, insurance companies, even stock brokerages. The thin line that separates banks from other types of financial institutions is growing increasingly blurry. The latest banking legislation makes it even more difficult to separate banks from other types of financial institutions. Whether this is good or bad, remains to be seen. In the meantime, the more you know about how each of these institutions functions and how each plans to take a little piece of your pie, the more skilled you will become in making the best of what you've earned.

As far back as the earliest days of our country, government officials agonized and debated over the shape that should be given to our banking system. They knew that banks would come to wield awesome financial power. In those days, it wasn't clear whether this power should be concentrated in a handful of institutions or whether it should be spread out among many. Alexander Hamilton was among those who felt that a single central bank was the best solution. Another great name in our history, Thomas Jefferson, was appalled at such a thought. He argued that local control was the only way to keep banks from becoming financial nightmares.

The ideas of both men were incorporated at various times in our history. Gradually, our banking system has evolved into what might be called a compromise between those two extremes.

Today, we have a wide range of banking institutions, large and small. Some are chartered by the federal government, some by state governments. All of today's banks are carefully regulated by federal and/or state governments to ensure that they properly and safely serve the public need. The huge Federal Reserve Banks control the money supply at a national level while the nation's thousands of individual banks hold sway over the flow of money in the communities they serve.

Because banks are such an important part of our economy and because their success hinges on maintaining the public trust, state and federal governments have passed many laws designed to ensure that our banking system remains sound. Time has proven that these efforts have been largely successful. The likelihood of a bank failure is far less today than at any other time in our history. And, because of federal insurance, the occasional bank failure does not result in the loss of individual depositors' money (up to the maximum coverage, which is $100,000 for each individual account at the time of this writing). Our federal government has also been key to the enforcement of nondiscrimination policies in banking practices by requiring equal opportunity lending.

Banks should not be thought of as evil, or even undesirable, institutions. If they didn't exist, we would surely have to invent them. Banks are important to us and they must be allowed to generate reasonable profits if they are to stay in business; a failed bank is a blot on our society and our economy.

So, it's important for you to gain a clear understanding of how banks work. That way, you'll be able to make full use of the essential services they offer without paying an unreasonable price.

In the next chapter, we'll be getting down to the nitty gritty in the important business of managing your money. Of course, before you can do a good job of managing money, you must first accumulate some money to manage. That brings us to the first (and perhaps most important) principle of personal financial management:

- **Always pay yourself first.**

Please read the above line again. It contains the four most important words in personal financial management. If you are to accumulate significant wealth, you must come to understand the importance of this principle. Put these words into effect now and you are on your way to greater personal wealth. Ignore them at your financial peril.

If you have ever said, "After I pay all my bills, there is nothing left to save," you are in dire need of emergency treatment. Pay close attention.

The shrewdest money managers understand the losing psychology of "back-door" savings. That is, putting savings aside only after all other needs are taken care of. That philosophy all but guarantees that there will never be anything left to save.

So, always pay yourself first.

Decide right now on how much money you intend to save each pay period and put that money aside first. What is left is what is available for you to live on. Even a small amount of money put away on a regular basis can grow to astonishing totals, thanks to the magic of compound interest.

***

Should you begin your plan for greater riches by drawing up a budget? Of course you should. Almost every book I've ever read on personal finance—and sometimes I think I've read them all—says that you must prepare a written budget at least once a year. In fact, many books contain elaborate forms already made up so that all you have to do is fill in the blanks. I've even seen books that say you must make out two budgets, one for the short term and one for the long term. Gimme a break.

You won't find any such forms here. Why? Because I know that you won't bother filling them out even if I go to the trouble of designing them for you, and even if I tell you that you MUST complete them. No matter what I say, you probably wouldn't fill out that budget.

No one I know personally will admit to making out a written budget. I understand that we're all supposed to do it, but I never have. And I've made out just fine, thank you. Please don't write to me about this. I'm well aware that you're supposed to go through this exercise, and I know that it's good for you. If you are a believer in written budgets, if you insist on making out a budget for yourself, that's fine with me. After all, it couldn't hurt.

If I ever meet Donald Trump, I'm going to ask him if he ever made out a written budget for his personal finances. Frankly, I doubt it. But if he says that he does it, I'll promise to start doing it too. In the meantime, I'll just continue building my wealth by following the principles I've outlined for you in this book.

***

O.K. So now you've saved a few dollars, or maybe you inherited them. Either way, it's time to learn how to get the most out of what you have. We'll start with banks. After all, the first place most people put their money is in a bank.

As you have seen from their history, banks have always been two-edged swords—faithful friends for the most part, but potentially dangerous enemies for the unwary. So, let's start out by taking a look at how you can beat the banks at their own game (or at least give them a run for their money).

CHAPTER THREE

Banks—Sleeping with the Enemy

I hesitate to deposit money in a bank. I am afraid I shall never dare to take it out again. When you go to confession and entrust your sins to the safe-keeping of the priest, do you ever come back for them?

—Jean Baudrillard (b-1929), French semiologist.

O.K. Banks aren't exactly the enemy. But don't confuse them with your kindly old uncle who is so concerned about your welfare. Banks are in business to make money, and they've learned how to carry out that assignment quite handily. Your bank will take as much of your money as the law will allow…and as much as YOU will allow.

Former banking executive, Edward Mrkvicka, Jr., estimates that you will likely overpay your bank, through mortgages, credit cards, loans, and checking and savings fees by more than $100,000 in your lifetime. Personally, I'm inclined to believe that Mr. Mrkvicka's estimate may be a trifle ambitious. Still, the lesson is clear: Your relationship with your bank is going to cost you money.

Fortunately, you have a great deal to say about how much money your bank will make off you…at least as compared to the next guy.

Banks are heavily regulated by federal and state governments, but the law gives them considerable leeway in both the nature and the cost of the services they provide. It's up to you to learn how to deal with them in a way that will allow you to maximize the benefit of the services they offer while keeping their paws off as much of your money as possible.

This is not an academic exercise. Over a period of years, a well-informed bank user will have a huge financial advantage over the poor klutz who lets the bank make financial decisions for him. Let's start at the beginning.

Banks love customers who open passbook savings accounts, and for good reason. Of all the types of accounts banks offer as safe havens for your money, passbook accounts pay the lowest rate of interest to the depositor. Said in a different way, it's the lowest-cost way for a bank to attract deposits. If you browse through those cute little brochures that your bank displays in its lobby, you'll find passbook savings accounts described in glowing terms (though they may call them by different names).

If your account comes complete with a passbook (or a monthly statement) into which is carefully entered each deposit you make, and you are allowed to withdraw your funds at any time (but not by writing a check), you have a passbook or statement savings account. If you have one, you are not alone. Millions of Americans who simply don't know any better have all or most of their money deposited in savings accounts in banks and savings & loan associations.

Now, consider this: The interest rate structure in most of today's commercial banks guarantees that you will **lose** money if you keep your savings invested in bank saving accounts. This curious situation is due in part to a phenomenon that you know about, but may not fully understand. It's called inflation.

In modern times, the average cost of the products and services that we must buy with our money has gone up each year. That means that each dollar will buy less next year than it can buy this year, and even less the following year. The rate at which prices rise each year is called the inflation rate and is expressed as a percentage. An inflation rate of 3%

means that the average cost of goods and services has risen by that much during the 12-month period involved.

Put another way, your dollar is worth only 97¢ in purchasing power after an inflation rate of 3%.

It doesn't take a mathematical genius to figure out that year-after-year of inflation means that the value of each dollar is being seriously eroded. And remember, we've had many years in which the inflation rate has been a lot higher than 3%. The inflation rate is reflected in what is known as the Consumer Price Index (CPI). Figure 1 shows the change in the CPI over the most recent 20-year period. Note that the CPI has increased in every one of those 20 years.

Consumer Price Index (CPI) Annual percent of increase 1980—1999				
1980	+12.5%		1990	+6.1%
1981	+8.9%		1991	+3.1%
1982	+3.8%		1992	+2.9%
1983	+3.8%		1993	+2.7%
1984	+3.9%		1994	+2.7%
1985	+3.8%		1995	+2.5%
1986	+1.1%		1996	+3.3%
1987	+4.4%		1997	+1.7%
1988	+4.4%		1998	+1.6%
1989	+4.6%		1999	+2.7%

Figure 1

A quick look at the chart will explain to you why it cost $2.19 in 1999 to buy what could have been bought for $1.00 in 1980. And we have no reason to believe that this spiral in inflation is likely to change for the better in the years ahead.

One of the primary objectives of your personal finance plan must be a determination to beat inflation. The only sure way to do this is to earn a rate of return on your investments that is higher than the rate of inflation—and the higher the better.

With that objective in mind, understand this: Interest paid on most bank savings accounts is usually lower than the rate of inflation. Thus, though there may be a few more dollars in your account at the end of the year, the total of those dollars will have less purchasing power than the dollars you had at the beginning of the year. In short, you have lost money by keeping your nest egg in a "safe" savings account.

If passbook savings accounts are such a lousy deal, why do they still exist? Why do so many people buy into them even though their shortcomings are so well documented?

Most likely, it's because savings accounts are the simplest, easiest to understand, and the oldest form of bank savings (not to mention the fact that banks are happy to promote them at every opportunity).

When it comes to money management, many people are downright lazy. Worse, many savers are intimidated by, or ignorant of, the relatively simple banking options available to them. If you will stick to the principles outlined in this chapter, you won't have that problem.

So, for openers, what should you do if you have ANY money in a passbook savings account? Simple. Follow our next principle of sound money management.

- **If you have any of your money in a bank savings account, close it out at once, and put your money in an account that will pay you a higher rate of interest.**

As you have undoubtedly heard, good money management calls for keeping a reasonable amount of money readily available for emergencies. Most financial advisors suggest that you should have enough ready cash to keep you going for about six months in the event that your normal source of income is cut off.

That's good advice. And that emergency fund must be kept in an account that will give you immediate access to it, without penalties. A bank savings account fulfills this requirement nicely, but the shrewd saver knows that there's a much better way to handle this need. Happily, it's available right at your own bank. It's called a money market account.

In all likelihood, your bank offers a money market account that pays more interest than a savings account, allows you to withdraw your money on demand, and may even allow you to write checks against it. To be sure, the improvement in interest will not be nearly as dramatic as it would be if you put your money into one of the other account types that we'll be discussing later. Still, good money management, the kind of management that will help to lift your financial status above the masses, calls for taking every advantage available to you without wasting time. Time, as they say, is money.

So, go to your bank, ask what interest your savings account is now paying (a good money manager would already know this). Then, find out how much more you would get by transferring that money to a money market account.

Don't worry if the difference in interest rates seems small. The following paragraphs will illustrate the importance of understanding the range of interest rates available to you. And you'll see how important it is for you—not the bank—to decide where and how your money will be left in their custody.

Let's take a look at one of the most common mistakes made by the average saver/investor. Many people, perhaps most, pay little heed to what seem to be minor differences in the rates paid among different types of investments and savings options.

As an example, let's say that you've decided to buy a home and will assume a $100,000 mortgage. Your broker has found a lender willing to provide a mortgage at the rate of 9% for 30 years. By the time you're ready to hold a mortgage-burning party, you will have paid back that $100,000 loan, plus $87,500 in interest. Sad but true.

Now let's say that after reading this book you decided to do your own shopping for a mortgage before signing on the dotted line. Let's say that you found another lender willing to give you the same mortgage but at a 1% lower rate—8% instead of 9%. With that mortgage, you'll be paying $25,100 less for the same house. All because of an interest rate that was only 1% lower than the rate you were first offered.

Now you know why the people who lend money are willing to dicker over as little as one quarter of 1% in the interest they will charge.

The good news is that interest works similar magic in the other direction as well. When you're on the receiving end of interest payments, it's every bit as important for you to shop around for the best possible rate.

Let's suppose your rich Uncle Jake left you $10,000 and you decided to stash it away in one of those bank savings accounts paying a paltry 1.5% interest. After 25 years, that $10,000 would grow to $14,547. Not bad at first glance. But wait. If inflation remained about the same as it is today, your $14,457 would actually be worth less (would have less purchasing power) than the $10,000 you had when you started. Adjusted for inflation, you LOST money.

However, if you had read this chapter and knew enough to put that money into an account that paid, say, 5% interest, it would be a much different story. After 25 years, the account would be worth $34,812— not a great investment, but far better, and a substantial profit over inflation.

***

Of course, in the real world, the above scenario would not take place. Inflation rates aren't likely to remain fixed over such a long period. Worse, in many states, leaving an account untouched for that long would risk losing it all. Once a bank account has been officially classified as inactive, it becomes subject to state laws. In some states, that could make it difficult, even impossible, for you to get your money back.

So, let's take Uncle Jake's $10,000 and use it to help our retirement. We'll put it in the bank and add $100 each month for 25 years. At 1.5% interest compounded monthly, we'll wind up with what appears to be a tidy $50,964. But don't be fooled. When inflation and the total amount of money we've deposited are taken into account, we've gained no ground at all. In fact, we've again lost money.

Of course, we're too savvy to let that happen. Instead, let's put that money into a money market account at 5%. After 25 years of faithful saving, we'd have a tidy $94,610—a huge difference, and a healthy gain over inflation.

These are theoretical investments. They serve just one purpose. They're intended only to illustrate how seemingly insignificant differences in interest rates can produce dramatic differences in the result over long periods. There are far better places than money market accounts to put your money over the long haul. We'll be taking a look at many of them later. In the meantime, please consider the next important principle of sound money management:

- **Whether you are paying interest or receiving interest, never be satisfied with the first offer you receive. Shop around before you sign.**

And "shop around" means exactly that. Bank deregulation has produced a competitive environment with wildly different interest rates and bank charges. If you can get a better deal than your present bank is offering, take it. There is absolutely no reason for you to stick with a bank that isn't competitive. Remember: It's your money.

The best investment accounts available through most commercial banks are called certificates of deposit (CDs). CDs are a form of account that requires you to commit your savings for a specified period. That is, you will be charged a penalty if you withdraw your money before the maturity date that you specify when you open the CD.

Typically, CDs can be opened for periods of 90 days, six months, or one, two, or five years. Each of these maturities will yield a different interest rate, depending on the current interest market and local competition. Generally, the longer you are willing to leave your money in a CD, the higher rate of interest it will return, though this is not always true.

One popular way to gain maximum advantage in this system is to break up your total investment kitty into several equal parts and invest them in CDs with staggered maturity dates. Carefully planned, this approach can allow you to take advantage of high interest rates while ensuring that a maturing CD and its penalty-free cash are never very far away.

***

Once you begin to invest part or all of your nest egg in CDs, you will soon have to deal with the issue of what to do when maturity rolls around. It is likely that your bank will do a dependable job of sending you a reminder as each CD approaches its maturity date. It's also likely that the notice will carefully explain that you don't have to do anything at maturity if you don't want to. If the bank doesn't hear from you, they'll just "roll over" the CD. That is, they'll renew it for the same period as the original and pay you their current interest rate.

Sounds fair enough. It's easy and convenient. That's why millions of today's busy people take that easy road. The banks love people like that, but those millions of people are making a mistake that you can and must avoid.

Every person I've asked who allows CDs to automatically roll over at maturity has told me the same thing. They just assumed that the bank would see to it that they would receive the best available interest rate. That seems logical enough. A good customer willing to leave it up to her bank to make investing decisions for her will surely be well-taken care of. Right?

Wrong. I learned that lesson after some bad experiences at several local banks some years ago. The last straw came in the form of a renewal notice that my substantial one-year CD had been renewed at 3.5% interest. This at a time when competitive rates were running a little over 5% for one-year CDs.

I called the bank and asked to speak with the branch manager. I made it clear how unhappy I was with the outlandish interest rate they had assigned me, and guess what? Despite the fact that my renewal had already been processed and theoretically could not be changed, the manager somehow found a way to get it done. He canceled the renewal and gave me a special 13 month promotional rate nearly 50% higher than I would have received from the automatic renewal for 12 months.

I'll bet that you can already see the next important financial management principle coming:

- **Never, NEVER allow your CDs to renew automatically. Always call or visit the bank and ask to review all current interest rates for CDs, including any promotional rates that might be available.**

That's right. Banks often run special promotions offering interest rates higher than their regular rates. You can be sure that an automatic renewal won't be given that rate. Always ask.

By reviewing all the rates, you also have the advantage of seeing how much more interest you would receive if you signed up for, say, two years instead of one. Depending on current financial market conditions, the differences between longer and shorter maturities can vary considerably.

Finally, if you are fortunate enough to have substantial amounts available for investing in CDs, say $50,000 or higher, always ask about so-called Jumbo Certificates. Many banks offer rates that are a notch or two higher for certificates that meet their minimum requirements. Again, it's been my experience that they won't tell you unless you ask.

***

Keeping a lid on bank charges.

Your relationship with your bank involves money flowing in two directions—from the bank into your accounts and (ugh!) from your accounts into the bank. Your job is to maximize the former and minimize the latter.

Banks made an astonishing $5 billion in 1999 from bad check charges. According to Debt Counselors of America, this is partly because some Americans forget to charge their debit card purchases to their accounts, thus creating an overdrawn condition. Debit cards may look like credit cards, but the resemblance is strictly superficial. More about debit cards later.

When National City Bank in Pittsburgh imposed a $2 fee for deposit slips, their customers went wild. Enraged depositors were screaming and throwing things at stunned tellers, reported the *Pittsburgh Gazette*. *The bank soon ditched the fee, proving once again that bank customers don't have to suffer the indignities and mistreatment that some bankers seem to enjoy inflicting on them.*

In another, largely invisible, ploy, some banks make it a policy to process the largest check first. Let's say you accidentally overdraw your checking account. You have $300 in the account and you write three checks in one day. The first is for $10, the second for $20, and the third for $350. Some banks process such checks not in the order received by them but in order of size. The result in this case: The $350 check would be processed first. That means all three checks, not just one, would bounce and you'd be hit with three separate bad check charges. Besides an overdrawn account, you'd be out as much as $105 in painful overdraft charges (some banks are now charging $35 for each overdrawn check).

If you think that sort of thing doesn't happen often, you'd be wrong. Banks take scant pity on the consumer who is careless enough to overdraw a checking account—and $5 billion a year in revenue isn't to be treated casually. The smart money manager makes sure that not a dime of that money comes out of his pocket. So, our next principle of sound money management is:

- **Train yourself to avoid overdrawing your checking account. Writing a check for more money than you have in your checking account is a harmful folly as well as a costly mistake.**

But don't fall for that overdraft checking gimmick. If your bank tries to sell you on the idea of opening up an overdraft checking account, tell them to forget it. Sure, they'll lend you the money to cover any accidental overdraft that you might make. In fact, they'll be happy to take care of it for you as often as you like. But you'll pay an unconscionably high interest rate for short-term loans and your friends at the bank will love you even more.

In recent years, increasing numbers of banks have stopped paying interest on the money held in checking accounts. If your bank is one of them, your job is to keep the least amount of money possible in your checking account while making certain that you never overdraw the account. Here's a little trick that will allow you to safely and conveniently come out the winner. It's my next principle of sound money management:

- Open up a money market account at the same bank that has your checking account. Ask the bank to link the two accounts so that you may transfer money between them by telephone. Most banks now also permit money transfers online.

From that point on, never make a direct deposit into your checking account. Make all your deposits into the money market account where they will immediately begin drawing interest. Keep the minimum amount in your checking account and transfer money as needed to cover the checks you write. This is one of the smartest ways to maximize your regular operating funds, but don't expect to hear about it from your bank.

**

If you've been around for a while, you may remember when those newfangled Automatic Teller Machines (ATMs) were first introduced by your friendly bank. You didn't take to those new gadgets at first, and your bank was more than a bit concerned about that. After all, if they could persuade you to use those little machines instead of standing in line to do business with a live teller, they stood to save a lot of payroll money.

So, the banks embarked on extensive advertising campaigns designed to persuade you to help them lighten their payroll load. Of course, they didn't put it quite that way. Instead, the ads trumpeted how convenient and time saving it would be for you to use an ATM instead of bothering to visit a live cashier. What's more, this new service would be entirely FREE.

You (and millions of your fellow citizens) took the bait. In time, ATMs became almost as familiar as stop signs. There are now about 200,000 of those cash-laden machines scattered throughout the country.

It wasn't long after the machines came into popular use that the predictable happened. Once you and I became hooked on ATMs, the banks came to regard them as a generous gesture on their part—an essential service that they offered to their customers solely because of their burning desire to serve the public good.

Then one day, some anonymous bank executive had a brainstorm. Why not levy a charge on your account whenever you use an ATM owned by a bank other than your own? Once the word got around, just about every bank in town jumped on the bandwagon. At last count, nearly 90% of banks are assessing ATM surcharges. The widespread fees now average from $1 to $2 per transaction and you can be sure that they will rise as more banks come to regard ATMs as profit centers.

This outrageous policy so inflamed ATM users that public pressure and, in some cases, legislative edicts have halted or slowed the practice in some areas. In late 1999, the city of Santa Monica, California became the first municipality to outlaw surcharges for using ATMs. This legislation is sure to be copied by other cities and towns. The Defense Department recently proposed banning ATM surcharges at all domestic military installations. In most areas, though, the charges still prevail. Whether or not legislative action will prove to be a permanent solution remains to be seen.

Personally, I solved the ATM issue quite nicely, thank you. And I highly recommend that you do the same. I simply cut up my ATM card and resumed that old-fashioned practice of stepping inside the bank to transact my business.

Is this an unthinkable step backwards? Would it be a frightful inconvenience for you to do without ATMs? If you think so, I insist that you disabuse yourself of that silly notion at once.

To begin with, dumping mine was a marvelously liberating experience, requiring nothing more than a slight change in my timing. Once you accept the fact that you must arrange your schedule so that you visit your bank during banking hours, the battle has been won. With the extended banking hours offered by most banks these days, the whole process is a non event. In fact, I often find that the line waiting to use the ATM machine is longer than the line inside the bank.

And don't forget those untidy muggings that seem to be taking place at more and more ATM machines. Doing business inside the bank means that the only muggers you'll have to worry about are behind the desks. Remember, too, that the limitations in liability if your credit card is stolen do not apply if someone gains access to your ATM card and PIN number. Your account could be cleaned out before you know what's happened, and you may have little if any recourse.

However, if you're so hopelessly addicted to ATMs that you turn numb at the thought of going cold turkey, there is still hope for you. Check out www.freeatms.com or www.atmsurcharges.com on the Internet. These sites provide lists of ATMs all over the country that are no-charge, even for people who are not customers of the bank involved. However you do it, don't allow yourself to be charged for withdrawing your own money from your bank.

And there's yet another solution (sort of). More than three-quarters of the banks now allow you to use your ATM card without a surcharge at point-of-sale terminals such as grocery stores. Just pay for your purchase with your ATM card and be sure to get some extra cash at the same time. *Voila!* Cash without a fee.

***

Chances are that you are quite familiar with the wave of bank mergers that took place during the 1990s. In fact, you've probably been a victim of merger mania at least once. That's when you wake up one day to find out that the bank you've been doing business with for years, the bank that you chose yourself, is no longer around. It's been merged with another bank that has laid claim to you and your accounts.

Will this new bank, which is now larger than the gross national product of some countries, treat you better? Will it exercise economies of scale in order to bring you bigger and better services?

Forget it. Experience has clearly shown that the huge megabanks resulting from merger mania are raising inefficiency and customer alienation to undreamed of heights.

No, this isn't the work of arch criminals intent on robbing us blind. It's simply the classic symptom of unwieldy bureaucracies grown to a size that defies the best of management intentions. You see it all around you. Huge corporations that have somehow erected an impenetrable wall between the occupants of the ivory tower and the customers who pay their enormous salaries. It's one conundrum of modern business life that no one has yet been able to solve. Now, with new laws blurring the line between banks and other types of financial institutions such as insurance companies and stock brokerages, the financial behemoths can only grow even larger.

Gigantic Merrill Lynch, the world's largest brokerage firm was the first to take advantage when Congress killed the 1933 Glass-Steagall Act. That law was originally passed in an effort to keep brokers and banks from invading each other's territories. Once the way was cleared, Merrill Lynch announced that it would begin offering a federally insured interest-bearing bank account to its customers. That was a direct challenge to banks and S&Ls for some of the $4.1 trillion tucked away in savings deposits.

This move, soon followed by other large brokers, makes it even more difficult to distinguish a bank from a brokerage firm, from an insurance company.

Fortunately, you don't have to solve this frustrating problem yourself. All you have to do is make your best effort to avoid it. Fortunately, that's not hard to do. All of which brings us to the next principle of sound money management:

- **Search out the smallest FDIC member bank in your neighborhood and give it your business.**

They'll be happy to have you as a customer. They need you and they will appreciate you. You'll receive a lot more personal attention from a small neighborhood bank than you ever will at a financial behemoth.

And don't wait. If you don't support your small neighborhood bank, there soon won't be any small neighborhood banks. If that happens, you'll be the loser.

Even at a small bank, you'll still have to follow the principles outlined in this chapter. But you'll be doing it in a friendlier atmosphere. Fewer banking frustrations will leave you better prepared to enjoy your stroll down the path to greater riches.

CHAPTER FOUR

Where Else Can I Stash My Cash?

'Tis money that begets money

—Old English proverb

There are only two places in which many Americans, perhaps most, are willing to keep their money—in their pockets or in the bank. Despite the protests of many investment gurus, that's actually the most sensible financial philosophy for SOME individuals.

Barbara is an elderly widow who lives by herself in the home that she shared with her husband for over 40 years. Like many wives of her generation, she left household financial matters entirely to her husband, a corporate executive. When her husband died, Barbara found herself overwhelmed with the complexity of their financial investments.

It was a struggle for Barbara at her time of life to learn even the basics of certificates of deposits, money market accounts, and other services available through her local bank. Stocks, bonds, even mutual funds were concepts that she simply wasn't prepared to deal with. Still, 10 years after her husband's death, her net worth, adjusted for inflation has risen significantly. Barbara has kept all of her money in several banks, following the general principles outlined in the previous chapter. The result has been reasonable financial growth with a minimum of emotional stress.

If Barbara had been able to find a trusted relative or friend who understood investments, and who was willing to take over the management of her portfolio, she could no doubt have done much better. Short of that, however, sticking with bank investments was Barbara's best choice.

Then there was my mother-in-law, mentioned earlier. Unlike Barbara, Elizabeth was the financial manager for her family from the beginning. Despite a modest family income, Elizabeth used her instinctive money management skills to support a life style that belied their family's position on the economic ladder. When she died at the age of 98, Elizabeth had accumulated a tidy nest egg that placed her net worth well above the average American. Yet, she never invested a cent of her money anywhere except banks and savings and loans. While Elizabeth had and employed solid financial instincts, she did not understand, nor would she have trusted, stock and bond investments.

And there are other circumstances that make banks the best place for SOME people to invest their money. Investments in the stock market, real estate, and individual business ventures all pose significant risk. While the potential rewards are greater than those offered by relatively tame bank investments, it's also possible to lose some, or even all, of your money in such investments.

Some people have an extremely low tolerance for that kind of risk. Emotionally and psychologically unsuited for the stress involved in the ups and downs of volatile investments, such people should completely (or mostly) avoid any but the safest of insured investments. The potential premium offered by stock market investments simply isn't worth the grief that risk-averse investors would put themselves through by agonizing over the ups and downs of the market.

Further, until you have a solid base of savings in bank investments, say $10,000 or so, you shouldn't even be thinking about alternatives. You need to know that you have enough in insured savings to see you over any tight spots that might develop before you start risking any of your capital. Which brings us to the next principle for sound financial management:

- If investments that pose a risk of loss of capital would cause you to lose sleep or snap at your spouse, go back and read Chapter 3 again.

Having fulfilled my responsibility to the economically timid, I must now advise you of the conventional wisdom involving personal finance and investment.

While it is possible—even easy—for you to build a respectable nest egg without traveling any farther than your local bank, there's something else you need to know:

It's most unlikely that you will ever be able to build substantial wealth without investing in instruments that pose some degree of risk. Perhaps more important, a portfolio completely devoid of such investments is an easy target for that economic demon that we call inflation.

One of the most damaging things about inflation is that it cleverly masks itself in unadjusted dollars. Here's what I mean.

If you buy a five-year $10,000 CD at 5% interest and reinvest all dividends, compounded monthly, you'll get your $10,000 back plus $2,836 interest in five years. That's a total of $12,836 for your original investment of $10,000. Not bad, at first glance. But let's take a closer look.

If we assume an average 4% inflation rate during those five years and the 28% tax bracket for you, that $12,836 will have less after-tax purchasing power than the original $10,000 you started with. In other words, you've actually lost money—nearly 1% per year—even though you have more after-tax dollars to count. That, my friend, is inflation.

There is no way I know of to foil the inflation devil without putting at least some of your money in investments that are likely to outpace inflation. Most common stocks have proven that they can do exactly that. Bonds have also been shown to beat inflation over the long haul, but to a significantly lesser extent than stocks.

Since most companies are able to raise their prices to compensate for inflation, they will usually be able to maintain their profit levels over long periods. That, in turn, means that stock prices are likely to rise in proportion.

For most people, the only non-bank type investments that should be considered, other than individual stocks, are bonds, mutual funds and, perhaps, real estate. We'll discuss each of these separately.

Perhaps the most important thing to remember about risk is that there is no way to make your money completely safe from it. Once you understand how inflation works, you realize that simply leaving money in the "safest" most "risk-free" investments available almost guarantees that you will lose purchasing power. Over time, you may have more dollars to count, but the ravages of inflation can make those dollars worth less in purchasing power than you had when you started. Some people are so consumed with the hoary exhortation to protect their principle that they wind up keeping their money in investments guaranteed to result in the very thing they fear the most. You should always remember the next principle of sound money management:

- **Conserving purchasing power is more important than protecting principal.**

Since there is no way for you to escape from risk, the best alternative is to learn how to manage it—how to keep it within boundaries that are comfortable for you. And that's one of the objectives of this book and its principles of sound money management.

***

Among the more popular options for investors who manage to accumulate a portfolio of at least $20,000 or so are the asset management accounts, sometimes called sweep accounts.

For a reasonable annual fee, these accounts available through many brokerage firms and banks allow you to combine all of your investments into one account. You get interest-bearing checking, easy purchasing and selling of stocks, mutual funds, bonds, or CDs and a particularly nice feature called sweeping.

In such an account, any uninvested cash that accumulates in the account from interest, dividends, stock sales, or deposits gets automatically "swept" into a short-term money market fund that pays the going interest rate for such accounts. This is a particularly attractive feature since it ensures that you never have cash sitting idly and not drawing interest.

Also, CDs purchased through your broker will usually bring you significantly higher interest rates than may be available at your local banks. This is possible because the brokerage firm is able shop the country to find the best CD deals.

Your broker or bank can tell you about their all-in-one asset management accounts. If you have sufficient funds to meet the minimum requirement, this may be a good choice for you. Be aware, though, that opening such an account will hook you up with a broker representative who will make money from your account only if you do a little buying and selling of securities.

***

There are, of course, any number of investments other than those mentioned here. Most of them, however, are suitable only for the more sophisticated, reasonably wealthy investor. These include such instruments as commodity futures, financial futures, preferred stocks, real estate investment trusts (REITs), stock puts and calls, and the like.

If you are a sophisticated enough investor that you already knew everything you've read in this book so far, you should put the book down and go on about doing your thing. If you aren't in that class yet, keep reading and stay away (for now) from any non-bank investments except stocks, bonds, mutual funds or possibly real estate.

If the day should come when you are ready for those other more complex investments, you'll know it. You won't need me or anyone else to tell you. Frankly, most people will never be ready, and it would be unfortunate for them if they got the notion that they were. In particular, I urge you to keep your distance from futures, either commodity or financial. Unless you are a skilled, full-time investor in futures, you have no business ever touching them. If you don't know what futures are, I'm not going to tell you. You should drop me a note and thank me for that.

**

The difference between stocks and bonds is as simple as the difference between a lender and an owner—or the difference between debt and equity. When you buy stock in a company, you are literally buying part ownership in that company. You have bought what is known as equity in that company.

To be sure, buying stock in a large public company will give you only an infinitesimal piece of the action, but it makes you an owner nevertheless. You will share in the success or failure of the company (and the resulting ups and downs in its stock price) to a degree proportionate to your investment. For many years, stock prices have appreciated an average of about 12% per year, even higher during the past few years. If you check the rate of interest on your bank-type investments, you'll appreciate what 12% could do for you and your future.

When you buy a bond you aren't buying ownership. You are simply lending your money to the issuer of that bond, whether it is a corporation, a municipality, or the federal government. That's debt money. The issuer of the bond owes you money, but you have no equity in the organization. Instead, in return for the use of your money for a specified period, the issuer agrees to pay you a specified rate of interest.

In general, stocks (equities) are regarded as more volatile than bonds. That is, stocks offer higher potential for both capital gains (increases in the stock's price) or losses (decreases in the stock's price).

Bonds are considered the more conservative investments. They offer a fixed rate of income and less chance for significant appreciation or loss. Keep in mind though, that the worth of your investment in either stocks or bonds can go down as well as up. In other words, these investments offer you more opportunity for growth and income than insured bank investments. At the same time, they pose the risk of loss of some or, in the worst possible scenario, all of your capital.

Stocks

In all likelihood, any financial advisors you consult with will tell you that the average investor should invest at least part of his portfolio in common stocks. And rightfully so. The reason is simple enough: For many years, stocks have provided the best overall return of any investment available to the average investor/saver.

For more than 60 years, the average return on stock investments has been 10% to 12% per year. For the past five years or so, from 1995 through 1999, it has been an astonishing 20%. These figures are there for everyone to see and it would be difficult to take issue with them.

But please keep two things in mind. First, past performance is never a guarantee of future performance. Second, remember that the **average** return is one thing, the return you will get if you start investing in stocks may well be—will probably be—something quite different. Remember, too, that during decades of rising stock prices, there have been occasional years when returns were abysmal and some where sharp losses hit nearly all investors. Still, over the long term, stocks are regarded as one of the best ways to keep the inflation wolf away from your door.

If you decide to accept the conventional wisdom and begin investing in stocks, you will have made only the first decision, the easiest one, by far. Next comes the tough one: Which stocks should you buy?

That's the rub. While the **average** price for stocks may go up substantially in a given year, there will be many stocks that will see substantial drops in prices during that same year. Pick the wrong stocks and you may well have a disastrous year, even when the overall market average is reaching for new heights. Even if you don't have a catastrophic year, it is unlikely that the return on your individually picked stocks will give you an overall return that will match the market average.

While you won't hear it discussed much, the great majority of full-time professionals are not able to achieve returns equal to the market average on their own portfolios over an extended period of time. Picking all winners and avoiding all losers is as close to impossible as you can get in this life. If the professionals can't do it, what chance does the poor amateur have?

**

There are hundreds, perhaps thousands of books available that purport to tell you how to pick winning stocks. Every conceivable system from the most arcane to the childishly simple can be yours at your local library or bookstore. Many of them are seductive and seemingly unassailable in their apparent logic. My own feeling about that peculiar phenomenon is that anyone who has discovered the magic key to stock market wealth isn't likely to toil for months or years writing a book telling every Tom, Dick and Harry how to grab a piece of his action. If he's so smart, why isn't he cruising the Caribbean on his 90-foot yacht instead of slaving over his word processor in Syracuse in December?

And that, Dear Reader, is why I believe that the ordinary investor, especially a beginner, should never attempt to invest in individual stocks. The smart way to enjoy the wealth-building potential of investing in stocks at the least risk is through a vehicle known as mutual funds.

Mutual Funds

To be sure, there is a lot of personal satisfaction to be had from selecting and buying individual stocks. First, there is the emotional tie that develops when you analyze a company's financial reports, taste or feel its products, or just thumb through the annual report basking in that feeling of proprietary interest. And what could compare to the emotional high that comes when one of your picks turns out to be a real barn-burner?

Unfortunately, unless you happen to be the second coming of Warren Buffet, the gaps between those highs are likely to be filled with a discouraging allotment of wallet-busting lows. When those lows come two or three at a time, the investing landscape can suddenly become a very lonely place. Enter mutual funds.

Do I own individual stocks? Yes, I do. Quite a few of them, in fact. But if I were to do it over again, knowing what I know now after 40 years of hard-won lessons, all of my equity positions would be in mutual funds. All of them.

The idea behind mutual funds is poetically simple. Made possible by the Investment Act of 1940, each fund is set up as a separate investment company. Each fund has its own management team and investment philosophy. When you invest in a mutual fund, you pool your money with a large group of other investors. A small part of your collective investment is spent to buy professional full-time management. The fund managers do all of the picking, choosing, buying, selling, and agonizing for you and your fellow investors. Since there are a huge number of other investors in your fund, only a tiny percentage of your own money is needed to pay for professional management.

Perhaps most important, buying shares in a mutual fund allows you to enjoy the benefits of diversification even if you don't have a lot of money to invest in stocks.

"If you build your portfolio out of mutual funds, somebody else will diversify for you," says Terence Odean, a finance professor at the University of California at Davis, quoted in *The Wall Street Journal*. *"You don't have to be emotionally attached to each stock in that portfolio. All you see is the big picture."*

Are mutual funds a foolproof path to stock market riches? Certainly not. The performance of individual funds can and does vary widely. Even the same fund can turn in an excellent performance one year and a miserable one the next.

Still, over the long haul, the advantages of investing in mutual funds can't be ignored. An amateur's tentative forays into the unforgiving jungles of Wall Street are simply no match for the full time attention of hard-nosed professionals who make the buying and selling of stocks their life's work. And so, you should heed the next principle of sound money management:

- **Resist the temptation to invest in individual stocks. Instead, put whatever portion of your portfolio that you have allotted for stocks into stock mutual funds.**

There is a special type of mutual fund called money market funds. These funds are similar to the money market accounts available through your bank, but they pay significantly more interest. However, unlike the bank version, money market funds are not federally insured.

As with other mutual funds, money market funds pool your deposits with those of many other investors. That money is then invested in high quality short-term government and corporate bonds. These funds allow you to write checks on your balance, making them like checking accounts that pay a respectable interest.

Money market funds are regarded as safe investments. However, you should be aware that the absence of federal insurance means that the risk of loss is always present.

Of course, even the investor in mutual funds has to make some important decisions…like what mutual funds should I buy. Since there are hundreds and hundreds of mutual funds now available on the open market, it might seem that you're no better off picking funds than picking stocks. But have heart; there's an important difference.

A major advantage of investing in mutual funds is the manner in which the funds are categorized into generic groups. Do you want to limit your investments to conservative blue chip stocks? There are many funds that do exactly that. Or would you like to concentrate on small emerging companies with high growth potential but at a smidgen more risk? No problem. Would you like a fund that invests in a combination of conservative and growth stocks? There are lots to pick from.

Even if your tastes run to the more exotic like stocks of companies that have shown a good record for protecting the environment, stocks in foreign companies, or stocks limited to specific industries, there is a mutual fund to satisfy your need.

A relatively new idea in mutual funds is the index fund. An index fund seeks to emulate the performance of its namesake by buying shares of all stocks included in the index. For example, an S&P 500 index fund will include shares of all 500 stocks included in the Standard & Poors Index. A Dow Jones index fund will limit itself to shares in all of the 30 stocks that make up the Dow Jones Industrial Average.

Similar funds cover the other major stock market indexes. By their very nature, index funds preclude the kind of sensational performance that may be achieved by a more general fund whose incredibly smart— or lucky—manager winds up picking a big percentage of high flyers.

On the other side of the coin, the so-called passive index funds eliminate the anguished cries of investors who do poorly in years when the market as a whole enjoys huge gains.

Except for the most dedicated investors willing to spend countless hours evaluating fund performances, index funds are the way to go. Anyone who invested exclusively in index funds since they first became available has enjoyed huge profits.

So, how does the relatively inexperienced investor decide which funds to buy? Or even what the choices are?

There are countless publications dedicated to helping you decide where to invest your money. There are even magazines devoted entirely to mutual fund investing. But for the beginning investor with an eye to one day becoming a millionaire, there is only one choice for that initial publication. Which brings us to our next principle of sound money management:

- **Go out and buy yourself a subscription to *The Wall Street Journal*...and read it every day.**

While there are any number of fine financial publications, there are none as indispensable to the novice and professional investor alike. *The Journal* lists price fluctuations for every stock, bond, mutual fund and virtually every investment vehicle every day, and that's only the beginning. Its stories on people, places and things in the world of business and finance are the most timely and informative available anywhere. By reading *The Journal* daily, you'll gain a financial education that will be worth many times the modest cost of the paper.

In *The Journal* and other financial newspapers and magazines, you'll find stories and advertisements designed to help you pick the mutual funds best suited to your temperament and financial goals. You'll quickly learn that most funds are members of families. That is, each of the major fund companies offers a variety of funds, each designed to appeal to a different interest.

An excellent way to learn about individual funds and how they have performed in the past is to send for the free packets of information they offer. Don't be bashful. Call the toll-free number of several fund families and ask for their material. In no time, you'll get a clear idea of what is available and, more important, which funds seem best suited to your objectives.

Among the larger companies are Vanguard, Dreyfus, Neuberger & Berman, and Fidelity. There are, of course, many others.

***

If you do your homework before you buy your first mutual fund, you'll make an interesting discovery.

Have you noticed that some funds impose a sales charge when you buy their shares? That is, they levy a charge much like a broker's fee, over and above the cost of the shares you buy. This charge, called a "load," is usually expressed as a percentage of the sales price.

Let's say, for example, that you decide to buy 100 shares of a fund whose shares are selling for $10. Your total cost for the transaction will be $1,000. A load fund that levies a sales charge of 6% will charge you $60 for the transaction. With the keen sense of investment sense that you've developed by now, you realize that your shares will have to rise in value by 6% just for you to get even. But hold on, it's even worse than that.

The 6% charge will be deducted from your $1,000, leaving only $940 to be used to buy shares. So, your total cost is actually $60 for buying $940 worth of shares. You've actually paid 6.38% to invest $940. Now you have to wait for the share price in that fund to rise a whopping 6.38% just to get back to where you started.

That transaction is called a front-end load, a load that is imposed when you buy your shares. An even more insidious fee is the back-end load. This is a transaction fee that is not levied until you SELL your shares.

My introduction to back-end loads came some years ago when I allowed my attention to wander while I was discussing a fund purchase. Once I heard there was no sales charge, I went ahead and OK'd the buy. It was only when I thought about selling my shares after a nice gain in value, that I learned my lesson. I discovered that it was going to cost me 5% of the **appreciated** value to unload my shares. Suddenly, that tidy little profit didn't seem quite so tidy.

Now here's the good news. There is no need for you to ever buy any type of load fund. Most experts have concluded that load funds perform no better than their no-load counterparts. Clearly, then, there is absolutely no reason for you to ever get involved with load funds, ever. So:

- **The only mutual funds you should ever buy are no-load funds. Find out before you buy whether there is an initial sales charge or a back-end load. If there is, run, don't walk, to the next fund.**

While some funds charge front or back end loads (they may be called sales commissions or redemption fees) and some do not, virtually all funds charge management fees. While you should study the literature to familiarize yourself with the range of management fees charged, I wouldn't fret too much over the differences. What matters is the bottom-line performance of the fund. If you buy two funds and one returns 16% for the year and the other returns 6%, you'll know which was your best buy without a lot of analysis.

***

Once you decide to start investing in stocks, whether you choose to go it alone or take the easy route of mutual funds, it's time for you to start thinking about diversifying some of your money into other types of investments. And there are lots of choices. But one note of caution before we turn to the next chapter.

It's very important, as you have read, to keep an emergency fund of cash available. You don't want to be caught with a sudden need for cash that might force you to sell an investment in a down market. But please don't misunderstand what is meant by "cash."

Cash, to the skilled money manager means any form of investment or account that can be redeemed immediately with no penalty for early withdrawal. It does not mean hard currency stashed away in a desk drawer or a safety deposit box.

The only way that you can keep every possible dollar working to build your personal wealth is to make sure that you never keep anything more than pocket money lying around the house. In fact, that's our next principle of sound money management:

- **Any time you receive a gift of cash, repayment of a loan, dividend or interest checks, or any other form of cash money, deposit it in an interest-bearing account as soon as you can get to the bank.**

It has always amazed me how long some people will allow a check to sit around before they cash it. When that happens, the writer of the check benefits from the float, while the owner of the check loses the interest that it could be drawing. A foolish waste of money.

Idle cash may be fun to count, but it's not working for you while it sits idly in the kitchen cookie jar. Those dollars that you may have stashed around the house, just in case, can add up to a lot of earned income over a period of years.

CHAPTER FIVE

Rounding Out Your Investments

Sometimes your best investments are the ones you don't make.
—Donald Trump (b. 1946), U.S. businessman.

Diversification. That's one investment philosophy that will get no argument from your financial advisor, no matter who he or she may be. Diversification is the most basic form of financial common sense and it deserves your full attention.

When your grandmother said, "Don't put all your eggs in one basket," she knew what she was talking about. I hope you were listening.

Once your kitty has grown enough to allow you start investing a few dollars in stocks or stock funds, it's time for you to start thinking about minimizing your risk by diversifying your investments.

Stocks are the first place you should look for capital appreciation, once you've squirreled away enough cash in the bank to cushion against unexpected setbacks and signed up for a tax deferred retirement account. But stocks are also the most volatile (subject to large swings up and down in price) of the usual investments. So, your first vehicles for diversification after you begin to invest in stocks should be bonds. That's right—bonds. I know that some people will tell you that bonds are too tame, but hear me out. I say that bonds are a great way to introduce yourself to a more sophisticated investing approach without jumping in with both feet.

Top quality bonds are less volatile than stocks (though they, too, can go up or down in price). Also, bonds often move in the opposite price direction from stocks, so they provide a form of hedging your bet. If you buy bonds with the intent of keeping them to maturity, interim fluctuations in their market value will be of no importance. You (or your heirs) will get all of your principle back at maturity.

Virtually all states, municipalities, school districts, public utilities and major corporations need to borrow money from time to time. The most popular and effective way for them to do this is by issuing bonds. When you buy a bond, you are lending the issuer your money in return for the promise to pay you a specified interest rate as well as the return of your full principal at the bond's maturity.

U.S. Government Bonds

As we all know so well, the federal government also needs to borrow money on a regular basis. They do this by issuing what are called Treasury bills, notes, and bonds. The only differences among the three are the maturity periods, with T-bills being issued for short periods up to one year, notes up to five years, and bonds for as long as 30 years.

While T-bills, notes and bonds can be bought directly through your regional Federal Reserve bank, most buyers find it more convenient to open up a brokerage account and buy them through the broker. Bonds you buy direct from the Federal Reserve are sold without a sales charge. Although brokers charge a small fee when they purchase "treasuries" for you, many investors feel the convenience is well worth the small cost.

Any way you buy them, government instruments are at the top of the safety pyramid because they are backed by the full faith and credit of the U.S. Government. You must have at least $10,000 to invest in "treasuries" and a minimum increment of $5,000 for higher amounts.

If you prefer the savings that can be had by buying your government securities directly from a Federal Reserve bank, there is a free instruction booklet available that will give you all the information you need.

Write to: Federal Reserve Bank of Richmond, Public Services Department, Box 27622, Richmond, VA 23261. Ask for the instruction booklet on direct purchase of treasury securities.

The U.S. Government also issues what are called zero-coupon bonds. These bonds generally pay a little higher interest than other government bonds. However, they pay all interest and principal only at the maturity date and nothing at all until then. Zero-coupon bonds are OK for investors who are confident that they will not need the money before the maturity date, and for investors who are confident that interest rates will not rise. Such confidence may be ill advised for the average investor. I don't recommend zeros.

U.S. savings bonds, like other forms of federal government bonds, are also among the safest investments you can make. And the Treasury has made it easier than ever to buy them. Series EE and inflation-adjusted Series I savings bonds can be bought at most banks and are now available online (www.savingsbonds.gov). Buy your bonds online and they'll be mailed to you promptly. You can buy a U.S. savings bond for as little as $25.

Keep in mind, though, that the convenience, low minimum purchase, and super-safety of U.S. savings bonds come at a price. On bonds issued after May 1, 1997, The rate of interest has been set at 10% below that of regular five-year U.S. bonds. That's enough of a difference for me not to recommend savings bonds except for the smallest, most conservative investor. If you have more than a few dollars to invest, you can get a better after-tax yield with other conservative investments such as regular treasury obligations or municipal bonds.

However, if you're just getting started in a savings and investment program, Series EE savings bonds shouldn't be ruled out. Prior to 1982 when the government made savings bond interest more competitive, they were among the worst possible investment choices. Now, with just a slight interest difference, a low minimum initial investment, and exemption from state and local income taxes, they represent a reasonable alternative to those ridiculous bank savings accounts.

Series EE bonds can be bought in denominations from $50 to $10,000 at a selling price of one-half the face value. An individual is allowed purchase up to $30,000 face value (total cost of $15,000) per calendar year. You can get the necessary forms to buy Series EE and the new inflation-adjusted Series I bonds from your local bank.

Corporate Bonds

The highest quality corporate bonds, rated AAA by rating companies such as Standard & Poors and Moody's, pay a tad more interest than U.S. Government bonds. One of the reasons for this is that most corporate bonds, unlike government bonds, are callable. That is, if interest rates drop, the issuer has the option of "calling in" the bonds and reimbursing the buyer at the face value of the bonds. The issuer can then issue bonds at a lower rate of interest thereby reducing its interest expense.

While this means that you won't lose any of your original investment. It also means that you will be "stuck" with unexpected cash for which you will have to find a home at a time when interest rates are below those in effect when you bought the bonds. It may seem unfair, but that's the price you pay for the slightly improved interest rate.

Your broker can tell you whether a bond is callable or not before you buy it. Sometimes the earliest call for a bond is far enough in the future to justify buying it. At least you know that you'll benefit from the stated interest rate until the call date rolls around. If the idea of having your bond called in disturbs you, stay away from callable bonds. There are other alternatives.

Municipal Bonds

If you are in the 31% or higher tax bracket, municipal bonds will return the highest after-tax yield of any high quality bond investment.

And they bring with them the devilish satisfaction of generating income shielded from the tax collector. If you live in a state that has an income tax, you can gain an added benefit by buying bonds issued by municipalities in your home state. These bonds are sometimes called triple-tax-free, since they are free of federal, state and local taxes. Generally regarded as the safest of municipals, a state's general obligation bonds are always a good bet.

Can you lose money on municipal bond investments? Yes, of course. Like any other bond investment, there is always the possibility of default. This is very rare, however, and isn't really a concern if you stick to bonds that are at least A-rated. Also, many bonds are insured against loss these days. Your broker can tell you about this.

Junk Bonds

Once you start shopping around for bonds, you're sure to notice the availability of bonds providing yields much higher than the going rate. For example, when high grade bonds are yielding an average of, say 8%, you may find some bonds offering yields of 12% or more. That's a huge difference, and there's a reason for it. The reason may be best illustrated by the term used to describe them. They're called junk bonds.

That nickname may be a little harsh; most junk bonds aren't really junk, but they do hold a higher risk than their blue-chip counterparts. When a company's credit rating is less than sterling, investors demand a premium when they buy the company's bonds; thus, the higher interest rate. In all interest-paying investments, the higher the rate, the higher the perceived risk. I have always held a junk bond or two in my portfolio. Over the years, I've enjoyed the higher interest rate without ever having a default. However, if you decide to put some small part of your portfolio into these high-yield instruments, please keep in mind that this is speculative money that conceivably could go down the drain.

Bond Mutual Funds

Since mutual funds are such a good idea for stocks, should you invest in bond mutual funds?

If the amount of money you have to invest in bonds is relatively small, say less than $25,000, bond mutual funds may be a satisfactory choice for you. The low minimum purchase required by most bond funds allows the small investor to accumulate substantial holdings gradually over a period of time. Also, bond funds continually buy and sell bonds, thus, unlike individual bonds, the fund has no maturity date. You can buy or sell a bond fund on the open market at any time.

Like their stock counterparts, bond funds come in a wide variety of flavors. High yield funds strive to attain highest income without unduly sacrificing safety. Growth and income funds strive for a performance that provides reasonably high current income with a good chance for price appreciation. Other funds limit themselves to bonds issued by small growth companies, foreign companies, municipalities, even government insured GNMA funds.

For the more sophisticated investor with larger amounts of money to invest in bonds, the funds are not, in my view, a good choice. Here's why:

Analyzing stock performance is a complex task, difficult for the average person to do effectively. Tangibles such as sales, profits, price-to-earnings ratios, product quality and industry performance must be factored in, along with intangibles such as consumer and investor confidence, when you estimate a stock's likely performance. The performances of bonds, on the other hand, tend to be influenced by a single economic statistic: interest rates. In general, bond prices move in the opposite direction of interest rates. When interest rates go up, bond prices go down, and vice-versa.

While it is difficult enough to predict the factors that influence stock prices, it is, in my view, next to impossible for anyone to predict future interest rates. Since all funds must pay a professional to manage them, and since even a professional cannot consistently predict interest rates, why pay for professional management? Management expenses for many bond funds have shown declines in recent years. Still, many experts feel that, unlike stock funds, the returns on bond funds do not justify the overhead expenses charged by the funds.

The major rating companies make it relatively easy and painless to select appropriate bonds for investment. Both Standard & Poors and Dow Jones publish quality ratings for most bonds available on the open market. If you stick to bonds that are rated at least AA, you'll have little to worry about in terms of the safety of your principal.

Of course the market price of the bond will decrease if interest rates rise after you buy your bond. That's no problem if you limit your bond investments to instruments that you expect to hold until maturity. You can thumb your nose at interest rate fluctuations if you don't intend to sell your bond before maturity. You'll continue to collect the stated interest and you'll get all of your principal back when the bond matures.

***

So, should you search the bond market (or any investment market) for the highest yields you can find?

Well, yes and no.

As long as you have money to invest, you must remember the next principle of sound money management:

- **In exchange for accepting a higher degree of risk, smart investors demand, and get, a premium in the form of a higher rate of interest.**

In plain English, this means that when you see a bond offering a higher interest rate than comparable bonds, you can be certain it is because that bond is seen as having a higher degree of risk. The extent of the risk will be reflected in the extent of the interest rate premium.

All of this has been said in even plainer English: "There's no such thing as a free lunch."

Bank CDs are a notable exception to all of this. All federally insured banks and savings & loan associations, large or small, carry the same federal insurance. So, when you're shopping for a CD, seek out the highest interest rate you can find and relax. Even if your local banks are so stingy that you have to go out of town to find a decent rate, go for it. Eventually, they may get the message. I live in suburban Philadelphia, PA, an area known for poor interest rates on CDs, compared to the national average. Why do our local banks get away with such a penurious policy? Simply because local savers, for whatever reason, seem willing to accept them. As long as they do so, the banks will be happy to oblige.

If you have access to the Internet, you may even want to ride the cutting edge by buying your CD online. E*Bank (formerly TeleBank), one of the first and largest of the growing number of online banks (www.ebank.com) consistently offers CD interest rates significantly higher than those available through conventional banks. And E*Bank carries the same FDIC insurance as its neighborhood counterparts. There are many other virtual banks, but be sure to confirm that the one you want to use is federally insured before you hand over any of your hard-earned dollars.

Today's banks, including online banks, are all but risk free. Government insurance protects individual accounts in each member bank up to $100,000. Persons with more than that amount to invest can put their money in several banks and maintain full insurance coverage at each bank.

Real Estate

For most people, real estate as an investment should not be considered until they have bought their own home. In fact, for most people, no investments of any kind should be considered until they are living under a roof that they can call their own.

Is buying a home really an investment? Should it be discussed in a chapter on investments? You won't have any trouble finding people who answer no to these questions. One school of thought says that buying a home is simply buying a place to live and that it shouldn't be regarded as an investment. I disagree.

I say that buying a home can be one of the best investments you will ever make.

Yes, yes, I know all about the weak housing market of the early 1990s and how some people lost money by selling their homes during that period. But, for the most part, that was an anomaly. For most of the past few decades, home prices have risen faster than inflation. For example, over the 20-year period of 1971 to 1991, average home prices increased by 6.6% (this, of course, varied by geographic region) while inflation averaged about 6.1% during the same period. That's not a super investment by most standards, but potential price appreciation is only one of the economic advantages, both tangible and intangible, of home ownership.

Remember my admonition to "always pay yourself first." When you take out a mortgage on your own home, payments on that mortgage are a form of paying yourself. Every payment you make adds to your equity in that piece of real estate, contributing to your growing net worth. On the other hand, every penny of rent that you pay is just more money down the proverbial drain. Meanwhile, your landlord is contributing to his growing net worth by using your money to pay down **his** mortgage.

Even without the price appreciation you can expect over the years, home ownership offers additional benefits that enhance lifestyles in a way that no other investment can. Your own home provides a feeling of security for you and your family, a healthy place to raise your children, and a feeling of self-confidence that comes from being a substantial part of your community.

On the investment side of the ledger, your home provides a hedge on inflation and some serious tax deductions. And the equity in your home can provide an excellent source of credit for such things as college education loans for your children. It's true when they say that your home will probably be the most expensive purchase you will ever make. But it's also likely to be the smartest purchase you'll ever make.

Is home ownership a risk-free investment? Of course not. But when you add up all of its advantages, both economic and emotional, it would be difficult to come up with an alternative investment offering a greater potential for enhancing your life. If you subscribe to the philosophy that buying a home should not be regarded as an "investment," that's fine with me. Whatever semantic description you choose to apply, I hope you won't turn your back on that cottage with the white picket fence.

In short, if you don't already own your own home, start planning right now to begin your shopping as soon as your finances permit. If you're already living in your own home, congratulate yourself on your shrewd financial acumen.

Precious Metals

I once attended a business meeting way back in the 1970s when I was employed by a large corporation. Several of us were given awards for one thing or another. Frankly I don't remember exactly what. What I do remember is the award. It was a one-ounce gold bar packaged in a handsome little envelope. I was thrilled. Gold at that time was selling for close to $700 per ounce. When I arrived home, I put it away. What a nice gift, I thought…and imagine how much it will be worth a few years from now.

I still have that gold bar, and now it's worth under $300—less than half what it was worth 25 years ago. I'm still delighted to have it, mind you. It's such a nice memento. But I wouldn't be nearly so pleased if I had used $700 of my own money to buy it 25 years ago. In fact, if I had sold that gold bar back then and invested the $700 in an account paying, say, a mere 5% interest compounded monthly, it would be worth about $2,200 today.

So much for gold, a commodity that many people will tell you is the ultimate investment and hedge against inflation. Gold, in fact, is so highly regarded as a stable worldwide medium of exchange that many advisors say that you should have perhaps 5% or 10% of your investments in gold or other precious metals at all times.

Not me.

The simple fact is that gold and most other precious metals simply haven't lived up to their reputations as investments. Like any other investment, the price of gold or other precious metals can go down as well as up. In addition, when you buy precious metals, you pay retail prices; when you sell you receive wholesale prices. In between, your investment sits returning no interest and racking up charges for safekeeping.

Except for that gold bar of mine, the most gold I own is in my mouth. That's the way I want to keep it.

Other "Investments"

You've probably read about the great investment potential of what some like to call "collectables." These may be anything from rare wines to stamps, coins, antique swords, Barbie dolls, old toys, guns, autographs, or any one of thousands of other do-dads. Forget it. Don't put a dime of your money into such objects because you think they are good "investments." Here's why:

To begin with, you'll be up against shrewd experts who know more about coins or toy trains than you'll ever know. Buying a "collectible" from some dealer or professional collector all but guarantees that you will never be able to get as much money out of your prize as you put into it. Remember. These people are making their living in the game. They couldn't survive for long if they allowed an amateur to walk in off the street and get the best of them. In the collectibles market, unless you are a professional, you will always pay retail prices when you buy and, if you're lucky, you'll get wholesale prices when and if you are able to sell.

There are only two exceptions to this advice:

First, if you are already an expert in the items you are collecting, then right on. You already know about what I've said in the above paragraphs and are no doubt hoping that this book doesn't get into too many hands.

Second, if you are collecting because you can afford it and genuinely enjoy whatever it is that you are cramming into your home and antagonizing your spouse with, go ahead and enjoy your hobby. But don't try to kid your spouse or yourself into believing that you are "investing."

There are any number of other investments that are perfectly legitimate, but they should be avoided until you have completely mastered the basics of investing. They include such goodies as Government National Mortgage Association Instruments (commonly called Ginnie Maes), Collateralized Mortgage Obligations (CMOs), and a host of far more esoteric investment vehicles. If you're still reading this book, you're not ready for any of them. Stick with the nuts and bolts for now and you'll be surprised at how well you will do.

***

Now that you have a good idea of the vast range of investments open to you, it's time to give some serious thought as to how to diversify your holdings among the different investments appropriate for your portfolio.

As is so often the case, some wise sage of long ago said it all more clearly and more simply than today's pedantic experts have been able to manage. Your grandmother's advice was so simple and so plain that I'm offering it to you as the next important principle of sound financial management:

Don't put all your eggs on one basket.

Once you clearly understand the need to diversify—to divide your "eggs" up into several different baskets—you must then decide how many eggs to put in each basket. That additional step is called asset allocation by financial professionals.

In the purest sense, that's all those two terms mean. Diversification is dividing your eggs up among several baskets. Asset allocation is deciding how many eggs to put in each of the different baskets.

Despite the sometimes painful elaborations that go into attempts to explain diversification and asset allocation, it all boils down to that simple aphorism that our grandparents understood so clearly. And you should too.

I'll use the terms diversification and asset allocation here because they are the terms you'll be seeing in all of your financial research and reading. But you should always remember the simple idea behind the terms.

Diversification and asset allocation in a planned and systematic way are vitally important parts of overall investment strategy. It's important that you understand the need for both, and that you consider them to be an ongoing part of keeping your financial plans in the proper balance.

Diversification is one of the reasons why funds are often a better choice than individual stocks or bonds, especially when you have a limited amount of money to invest. Most funds do a good job of diversifying within their specialized market areas while allowing relatively small investments.

To attain a suitable degree of asset allocation you should invest in a number of different financial instruments. This includes vehicles such as funds, stocks, bonds, CDs and other investments with which you feel comfortable. Further, you should aim for a sensible mixture of safe, conservative selections and those offering a bit more risk in exchange for a better chance of price appreciation or higher interest income.

You'll also want to balance your portfolio with investments that don't move up and down in price together or don't respond to the same economic influences. Stocks and bonds, for example, sometimes move in opposite directions, as do the stocks of big companies as compared to smaller emerging companies. The stocks of some companies are highly interest-rate sensitive, moving up or down sharply with changes in interest rates. Some stocks are known as cyclicals, because their stock prices and their financial performance tend to mirror cycles in the overall economy.

Every attempt at asset allocation, of course, should include a portion of cash or cash equivalents to meet emergencies. (Money market funds are considered cash equivalents since they can be immediately converted to cash without penalty.) Leaving part of your portfolio in cash or cash equivalents is a form of diversifying. Deciding HOW MUCH cash to keep on hand is a step in asset allocation.

So what should your asset allocation be? What percentage of your portfolio should be in stocks or stock funds vs. bonds or bond funds? Conservative vs. growth? International funds vs. domestic funds? How much cash or cash equivalents should you maintain?

You'll have no trouble finding published recommendations on this subject. Depending mostly on your age and the size of your portfolio, financial advisors offer a wide range of suggestions. Unfortunately, they sometimes differ markedly from one another even for people in the same circumstances.

Asset allocation is not a static equation. It will vary as you age, as the economy changes, and as your view of your objectives undergoes occasional revisions. That's why it's important for you to read a variety of current material on the subject and make sure that you constantly monitor your portfolio.

There are no right or wrong answers. What matters is that your diversification of assets suits your personal objectives; that it is under your control; and that it meets your psychological needs.

CHAPTER SIX

Credit—A Double-Edged Sword

*"I wasn't worth a cent two years ago,
and now I owe two million dollars."*
—Mark Twain (1835–1910)

My grandfather was very proud of the fact that he never bought anything on credit. "If I can't pay cash for it, I don't buy it," was his oft-repeated mantra. That's the way it was a couple of generations ago. Most people planned and saved in order to make major purchases. If they didn't have the cash in hand, they did without. For the right person at the right time, that can be a rewarding philosophy. But let's face it. These days, for most people, it just won't work.

My grandfather died in 1954. Life was far simpler back then. For one thing, credit cards didn't exist during most of his life. The idea of instant credit via a small hunk of plastic was unheard of by most people in those days—probably would have been rejected out of hand by many.

The major oil companies were the first to come up with the idea of instant credit. A few began offering credit cards for use strictly in their own gas stations in the 1920's. Then, one day in 1950, businessman Frank McNamara was embarrassed in a Manhattan restaurant when he forgot his wallet and couldn't pay for his dinner. He had to phone his wife to come bail him out.

Out of that experience came the idea for Diner's Club. In the first year, McNamara managed to sell, for a $5 annual fee, 200 Diner's Club cards. He had convinced 27 local area restaurant owners that it would help business if they would agree to accept the cards. Thus, the modern credit card was born.

In 1958, with those newfangled computers able to handle the complex billing chores, Bank of America issued the first widely used bank credit card. It was called BankAmericard, later renamed Visa. Today, there are 140 million credit card holders in the U.S. alone. Together, they owe more than half a trillion dollars in outstanding balances. The average American family with credit cards owed about $7,000 in 1997. New credit card purchases are now being rung up at the mind-numbing rate of more than $1 trillion per year.

***

Obviously, buy-it-now-and-worry-about-how-to-pay-for-it later has become the prevailing philosophy in American consumerism. Why wait for something you want if you have a good income and can make the payments?

Actually, there are lots of reasons. Where shall I begin?

My grandfather was right in his concerns about the dangers lurking beneath the surface of what was then our emerging credit system. Now, falling hopelessly in debt is as easy as saying, "charge it." Getting out of debt, as millions of people are now learning, is much harder.

Still, the reality of today's economic environment pretty much rules out my grandfather's anti-credit philosophy…at least for most people. The truth is that credit, used properly, can be a valuable tool for squeezing the most benefit from the money you have. But beware. The Credit Monster has ruined many lives. Credit can work for you, or it can work against you. That's why you should keep yourself keenly aware that credit is indeed a two-edged sword.

The dangers of improperly used credit probably can't be overstated. With credit card companies battling over the finite market for credit card customers, almost anyone can qualify for a pocketful of those little plastic squares that offer an easy portal into the land of milk and honey. Don't let yourself forget, though, that the bill ALWAYS comes. And a failure to pay what you owe when it is due can cause you more pain than a root canal.

The easy way to avoid the inherent dangers of the credit game would be to avoid credit entirely. However, even in the unlikely event that you could pull that off, it wouldn't be a smart decision. The smartest approach to credit is summed up in our next principle of sound money management:

- **Use your credit cards, but don't let them use you.**

As a rule, sound money management practice calls for paying your bills as close to the due date as possible. This allows you to take advantage of what is popularly called the "float." Using the float simply means that you keep your money in your own account as long as possible. That way, you benefit from the interest it draws for as long as possible, instead of allowing your creditor to benefit by sending in your payment before the due date.

All professional money managers work the float by paying their bills at the latest time that will not endanger their credit standing. In large companies, this need is obvious, since millions of dollars are changing hands on a daily basis. In your personal money management, the need may not be quite so obvious. After all, the interest saved will be in modest amounts. But don't lose sight of your target. Getting the most out of what you have calls for using every management technique that will enhance your overall financial well being. Small savings can add up to amazing amounts over long periods. By using this and other techniques described in these pages, you will develop a financial synergy that will be working for you around the clock.

But there is one pitfall to avoid when you are working the float.

In recent years, some credit card companies have become downright predatory in their late-fee practices. A twenty-five-dollar penalty for late payment is now imposed by many of the country's leading credit card issuers. That's a clear indication of how anxious they are for you to send them their money right now, so that they, instead of you, will benefit from the float.

Fair enough, but some companies have become downright cavalier about keeping up with the posting of payments received. In recent years, a number of consumer lawsuits have charged that some credit card issuers charge their customers late payment penalties even when the company itself is at fault by falling behind in posting payments.

That's reason enough to forget about the float when it comes to paying your credit card bills. It doesn't matter that you did the right thing. It doesn't matter that you mailed your payment to arrive a day or two before the deadline. Once those computers spring into their automatic charging mode, with penalty upon penalty added each month, you're in for nothing but grief until you eventually get the matter cleared up.

If you think that credit card companies aren't serious about taking a bite out of you whenever they can, consider this classic obfuscation recently sent out by a major credit card issuer to its customers:

> "Your account will be assessed a fixed annual percentage rate of 23.46% if in any Review Period (a) any portion of any minimum payment on your account is included within an unpaid minimum payment due on billing statements on three or more occasions, (b) any portion of any minimum payment on your account was included within an unpaid previous balance on two consecutive billing statements, (c) you breach the terms of any other [company name]

account, or (d) your account is considered in default for any reason and is canceled. The Review Period is the 12-month period preceding each billing period. Currently default accounts are assessed finance charges derived from a formula based on the applicable Prime Rate plus 13.99% if in any Review Period your account is in default as described in (b) or (c) or (d) above."

Trust me. I'm not making this up. That's exactly what they sent out. What does it say? Don't ask me. I'm just passing it along. One thing I'm sure of, though, it isn't a love letter.

So, our next principle of sound money management is:

- **Mail in your credit card payments as soon as you receive the bill.**

In other words, forget about using the float with credit cards. It's not worth the potential risk.

Besides, there's a better way to win at the credit card game. While having too many credit cards is an invitation to suffocation in a destructive web of credit card debt, even the most conservative user should have at least two credit cards. Here's why:

Let's assume that the billing cycle date for your credit card is the first of every month. If you make a major purchase on, let's say, the 28th of the month, you'll be receiving your bill in a couple of days.

Let's say also that you have a second credit card with a billing date of the 15th of each month. Now you have two cards with widely separated billing dates. If you decide to make a major purchase on the 17th of the month, you should use the credit card that bills on the 15th. That way, it will be almost a month before you receive a bill for the purchase.

This is a perfectly acceptable (and frugal) way to keep your money drawing interest as long as possible. All you have to do to adjust the billing dates on your credit card is call the toll-free number for customer service. I use two cards for personal use and two for business. I notate the billing date directly on each card so that I can whip out the right one when I make a large purchase. For convenience, I don't bother switching during a period of routine, smaller purchases. So our next principle for sound money management is:

- **Use at least two credit cards. Set up one for a billing date of the 1st of the month, the other for the 15th of the month.**

Of course, to enjoy the benefits of this sneaky system, you must pay off your full balance each month.

Did I mention that there is no other sensible way to use credit cards? Quite simply, if you are unable to pay off your credit card bills in full each month, you should cut them up and mail them back. Paying the minimum amount due on a credit card bill is a self-destructive practice, guaranteed to keep you in fiscal bondage forever. I'd rather see you borrow the money from your cranky father-in-law than slip into credit card slavery.

Millions of American families wind up paying as much for credit card interest as for the merchandise they buy. Put another way, paying the minimum amount due on a credit card is the easy way to pay twice as much for your purchases as other people pay.

Today's mail brought me a superb example of the seductive techniques that credit card issuers employ to snare the vulnerable and drag them into the credit quagmire. The teaser copy on the front of the brochure says, "Follow Your Dreams." Inside, the slick, beautifully illustrated pages shout such headlines as, Make the most of your credit card, Use your card to get the things you want. Use your card to follow your dreams. Make the most of life.

All of this is accompanied by tempting color photos skillfully designed to remind the reader of all the wonderful things the world has to offer…but only for those people smart enough to have and use their credit cards to the max.

Are you a sucker for this sort of mass hypnosis? I surely hope not.

***

Rotating your credit cards and mailing in your payments for the full balance promptly aren't the only ways to come out a winner in the credit card game. Instead of you forever paying your credit cards, turn the tables and make your credit cards pay you a little something in return. The Discover Card (800-347-2683) actually rebates part of the money you charge each year. You get a rebate of 1/2% on the first $3,000 you charge each year and an increasing percentage on amounts above that. It isn't much, but it's a sweet victory to see even a small part of your money finding its way back into your pocket.

An even more interesting deal is offered by Ford (800-285-3000) and GM (800-947-1000). Use their credit cards and you'll get a five-cent credit for every dollar you charge. The credits can be applied directly to the cost of a new Ford or GM car. For every $1,000 you charge, you get a $50 credit toward a new car. Now that's using credit cards the smart way. Instead of paying 18% or 20% in interest for everything you charge, get as much as 5% in after-tax dollars back.

By the way, do you have any credit cards that are charging you an annual fee for the privilege of using them to make the card companies richer? I hope you can see by now that it makes no sense at all to do that. There are any number of credit cards that will be happy to have you own them at no annual fee at all. When that annual fee next comes due, call the company and ask if they have a version without the annual fee. If the answer is no, cut up the card and return it.

***

No matter what credit cards you use, it's important that you get into the habit of carefully reviewing every charge on every billing statement.

Credit card companies and the vendors you buy from can and do make mistakes.

I have found many errors and improper charges on my accounts over the years. A recent example came to light when I noticed two charges, of different amounts, for gasoline from the same service station on the same day. Since I hadn't gone on any trip that day, there was no way I could have filled up twice. I called the credit card company to challenge the charge for which I had no receipt. The company removed the charge, "while they investigated." I don't know how that one was eventually resolved. However, I never heard from the company again…and I never went back to that service station again, either.

The most effective and easiest way to monitor your credit card charges is to get into the habit of saving every receipt from every charge purchase. When your statement arrives, check off each charge as you compare it to the receipt. This whole procedure takes only a couple of minutes a month and can save you a lot of grief. When you find a discrepancy, just call the customer service number on your card. Most credit card issuers are very cooperative when you challenge a charge. Of course, they will investigate, so you should always have your facts straight to avoid the embarrassment of having them remind you that you really did spend the money in question.

***

The days of low consumer interest rates are long gone. Today, if you borrow money, either through a direct loan or through the use of credit cards, you're going to pay a hefty price for the privilege. That's why it's essential for every borrower to know and understand the annual percentage rate (APR) charged by the lender.

Doing your own calculations to determine the true interest rate you are paying for a loan or for credit can be a numbingly complex process. That's why the 1969 Truth in Lending Law is so important to you. This law requires all lenders to disclose their true APR and the total dollar amount of their interest charges. This makes it easy for you to compare the true interest charges among lenders by comparing their stated APR. Always compare APRs among institutions in your area and among credit card companies. Take advantage of this easy way to determine your best deal.

Of course, it isn't always easy to determine the true interest rate on some credit cards. Some companies have become skilled in burying the details in rambling verbiage that very few people are willing to plow through. As this is written, there is talk in Congress about legislation requiring credit card companies to be clearer on their interest rates. Whether it will happen is problematic. Still, hope springs eternal.

When it comes to interest rates on loans, none is more important than the interest rate on the mortgage you take out on that new home. Besides shopping around for the best APR you can find, you must also consider the term of your mortgage. Many people opt for long-term mortgages of 30 years instead of the shorter 15 or 20 year terms. They do this because of the ill-informed notion that the smaller payments and longer term will make it easier to repay the loan.

If the smallest possible monthly payments are a critical need for you, the 30-year mortgage may indeed be your best choice. However, smart money managers know that short-term mortgages provide some very important advantages for those who can manage slightly larger payments.

To begin with, that new house is going to cost you far less money if you repay the loan in 15 years instead of 30. Let's say you take out a $100,000 mortgage for 30 years at 10%. Your monthly payments in that case will be $878. At the end of the 30 years, you will have paid the lender $316,000—$100,000 to repay the principal and a whopping $216,000 in interest. That's right. The interest alone on that $100,000 loan will be more than twice the amount you borrowed in the first place. Now you know why people are in the business of lending money.

Instead, let's say you followed the advice of many experts who recommend that you take out a 15-year mortgage. Now, your monthly payments will be higher. You'll pay $1,075 per month, only $197 per month more than you would pay on that 30-year mortgage. But take a look at the results.

At the end of your 15-year term, you will have paid $93,500 in interest. That means that your new house will cost you $122,000 less than it would cost under the 30-year mortgage.

Sure, you'd have to exercise a little discipline to squeeze that $200 bucks a month out of your budget. Still, if you have what it takes, you'll have taken one of the most important steps on your journey down the road to financial independence.

If a 30-year mortgage seems the only way for you to go, then it becomes even more important that you shop around for the best interest rate. On the usual 30-year mortgage, a reduction of only 1% in the interest rate will save you over $25,000 over the life of the mortgage. At that price, even a quarter or half percentage point is big money. The average borrower, anxious to get his loan approved, either doesn't understand this or simply "wants to get it over with."

So, our next principle of sound financial management is:

- **Always shop around to get the best interest rate for your mortgage, and take out the shortest term for which you can handle the monthly payments.**

Shopping around for a mortgage can be simplified if you use one of the mortgage-reporting companies to do the work for you. There will be a small charge, perhaps $25 or so, but knowing that you are getting the best mortgage deal around is worth many times that amount. I suggest that you call your banker or real estate agent and ask about mortgage-reporting firms in your area.

Many people simply don't understand the significance of a small difference in mortgage interest rates. A quarter-point or half-point difference doesn't seem worth bothering about. Lenders love people who feel that way.

If you're already locked into that long-term mortgage, it's still possible for you to give the mortgage boys a run for their money. Whenever you can, pay an extra monthly payment. If you did that only four times a year over the life of the 30-year mortgage discussed above, you would save a whopping $120,000 in interest charges. And that house would be all yours in 14 years instead of 30.

There is also the possibility of refinancing your mortgage if interest rates fall significantly after you take out your mortgage. There are many variables that must be considered in this decision. Such things as the number of years left on your mortgage, how long you expect to live in the house, and how much of a reduction in interest rates you can expect to get with a new mortgage. As a general rule, most experts suggest that refinancing will usually be to your advantage if you can get a new interest rate that is 2% or more lower than your present rate.

Refinancing under the proper conditions can result in a significant drop in your monthly payments (resulting from a drop in interest costs). Be careful, though, that you don't sign a new contract with a longer term than your original loan. If you do that, you could wind up doing more harm than good.

By now you're getting the idea. Understanding how interest works is an extremely important part of your financial education.

***

Borrowing money is a risky business. Once you get into the habit of borrowing money (except for a home mortgage) you are treading on the narrow edge of a deep precipice. Many people and businesses thrust into hopeless bankruptcy can trace the beginnings of their decline to unwise borrowing. In recent years, an average of one out of every forty families in the United States has declared bankruptcy.

At the very least, people who borrow unnecessarily often find themselves chained to the repayment of debt for the rest of their lives. Given that circumstance, financial independence is literally impossible.

Take the typical car buyer in this country. Many people find that they "need" a new car as soon as the last payment is made on their old car. So, payments on another car loan start as soon as the old loan is paid off. The result is a permanent loan—one of the most expensive kind—that often lasts the borrower's entire lifetime. This preposterous practice is so widespread that many people consider it perfectly normal.

Economists like to point out that you should never borrow money to buy a depreciable asset. That is, a product that goes down in value as time passes. Can you think of any asset that is more depreciable than a car? In general, it is said that a new car depreciates 20% in value the moment you drive it out of the showroom. If you doubt that, make a U-turn and try to sell it back to the dealer.

Among the newer clever ploys that the auto industry has come up with is the impossibly low interest rate. In its most common form, you will be given a choice of an interest rate on your car loan that is far below the current market or a cash rebate. A typical offer might be a 1.8% interest rate or a cash rebate of $2,000. If you get that offer, take the cash. Otherwise you'll be paying $2,000 more than your car is worth just for the privilege of a low interest rate.

It is important to understand that when you borrow money, you are paying more for the product than it is worth. That is, you are paying for the product plus the profit being made by the lender…and the longer you stretch out those payments, the more that item is costing you. The person who paid cash for that same item got it for much less than you paid. You know that wealthy neighbor of yours, the one that you're so envious of? You can bet that he didn't get rich by paying more for the things he buys than they are worth. The moral here is plain. Don't borrow money to buy something unless it is necessary that you have it.

But what is necessary? Do you really need that new TV, car, or vacation? More important, do you need them NOW? If you can afford to pay more than a product is worth in order to buy it now, congratulations. But why not pay yourself those monthly payments and buy the product for less when you've accumulated the necessary cash? Then you can put that left over money in your own account instead of the bank's.

It may seem that you are "doing without" if you put off such purchases, but are you, really? In time, avoiding debt will become second nature to you. The result will be your ability to afford far more luxuries than other people who have the same income as yours.

Following that advice, I guarantee you, will save you thousands and thousands of dollars over your lifetime—dollars that you can put to work in your program for building your own personal wealth.

***

Of course, in the real world, most people are going to borrow money at some time in their lives, probably many times. If you find yourself in that position, it is important to avoid the most damaging pitfalls in the treacherous world of the borrower.

When you borrow money, you will be required to sign a contract containing terms for repayment. If you take out a bank loan for this purpose (and whatever you do, never borrow money from a finance company) you should make it a point to read the contract. No, you won't understand most of it. It's written that way on purpose. That's why I want you to read it. The language you don't understand is taking advantage of you in ways that would make you ill if you did understand.

The typical legalese in a bank loan contract makes it possible for the bank to take everything but your soul if you default. Further, many contracts make it possible for the bank to call in the entire loan if you miss a single payment. Your failure to come up with all of the money at once will put you in default. If you can't come up with the money and the bank decides to sue, you've probably agreed to pay their lawyer as well as your own.

And these are just a couple of examples of an endless list of legal machinations that give the lender every advantage while giving you next to nothing. Do you still want to make that loan?

If you do, and I hope you do not, at least follow these suggestions:

Never borrow from a finance company. Not only will their contracts be at least as potentially destructive as the bank's; the loan will cost you more. Where do you think the finance company gets the money that it lends to you? It gets it from the bank or some other source that also has to make its profit. Get the idea?

Many people do not. That's why there are so many profitable finance companies around.

Knowing what you've learned about interest rates, can you believe that there are people in this world who actually borrow money on their credit cards. That's what you're doing if you fail to pay off the full balance on your cards each month; you're borrowing money at 18% to 22%.

Read over your credit card contract. Notice that little paragraph that mentions 1.5% interest per month? Sounds harmless enough doesn't it? But if you do your arithmetic you'll discover that 1.5% per month figures out to 18% per year, and some companies go even higher. Of course, the credit card companies know that almost no one will bother doing that calculation. That's part of the reason they continue to get away with such chicanery.

Can you imagine what your reaction would be if you went into your bank for a loan and the loan officer smiled and said we'll be happy to lend you the money…at 18% interest, or more? You'd probably stalk out in a huff. Still, when you allow a balance to carry over on your credit cards, you're falling into the same interest-rate abyss.

There are millions of credit card users who will never pay off their credit card debt. With a balance of $2,000 or more, minimum monthly payments will barely cover the interest charges plus minimal new purchases. Thus, the debt becomes a lifetime obligation. Our next principle of sound money management will steer you clear of that financially fatal error:

- **Always pay off your credit card purchases in full each month. If you can't come up with the cash at the end of the month, don't charge the purchase.**

Think of it this way: When you buy something on a credit card, you're actually borrowing the card issuer's money. If you pay off the full balance when you get the bill, you've borrowed that money at zero interest. You've beaten the opposition at their own game. You are one smart cookie. Doesn't that make much more sense than paying them 18% or more in interest in exchange for a little convenience?

Here's how one sage describes credit cards: "Little pieces of plastic that allow you to buy something you don't need, at a price you can't afford, with money you don't have."

Looked at that way, it kind of makes credit card junkies look a little foolish, doesn't it?

***

If you've already fallen deep into the credit card abyss, all may not be lost. But you must do everything possible to extricate yourself before it's too late. Shop for the lowest interest-rate bank loan you can find and pay off your credit cards. Whatever you do, though, don't go to a finance company or debt consolidator for your loan. If no bank will give you a loan, you may have already damaged your credit rating. If that's the case, maybe that brain surgeon brother-in-law will help.

No matter where you get the money, the loan you take out will still have to be repaid. But the lowering of your interest expense will at least give you a fighting chance for an economic recovery.

While you're paying off that loan, put your credit cards away for safe-keeping. Better yet, cut them into little pieces. Use them again and you'll wind up with TWO debts to pay off. You won't have any trouble getting new cards once you've developed a little self-control.

If you run out of ideas for getting out of credit card debt and nothing seems to work, check out www.fool.com/credit. This web site offers some good suggestions for working your way out of the credit abyss.

Buying a Car

If it's necessary for you to finance your next new car, please don't finance it through the dealer. Sure, it's convenient to let the dealer worry about all the "paperwork." And you can be sure the dealer will be delighted to arrange financing for you. Of course, he won't bother telling you that the reason for his accommodating nature is the generous cut of the action that he gets from the bank or other source of the loan.

And where do you think his cut comes from? You guessed it—from your pocket. The interest rate you pay on that loan will be increased to cover the dealer's piece of your pie. On a typical car loan at today's prices, you could be paying $1,000 to $2,000 more than necessary every time you finance a car through the dealer. Don't throw that money away. Instead, follow the next principle of sound money management:

- **If you are going to finance a car purchase, or anything else, go to your bank and arrange the loan yourself. You'll still get financially assaulted, but the pain will be considerably less.**

Whether you are speaking with a bank loan officer, a car salesman, or anyone else trying to sell you something, always remember the nature of the relationship. It's not that these people are your "enemies," or that they are out to "get" you. But a salesperson's perspective on the proposed transaction is always going to be very different from yours. What will serve the salesperson's best interests, even the most honest one, is seldom, if ever, what will serve your best interests. That's just the way the system works. In fact, most often, a salesperson's best interest will be in direct conflict with your own. Human nature being what it is, whose best interests do you think the salesman is going to try to serve?

No, salespeople aren't your enemies, but they are, in fact, your financial adversaries. It would be naive to think otherwise. In most cases, any optional or negotiated benefit that accrues to you must be taken away from the person on the other side of the desk. Keep that in mind whenever a salesperson makes you an offer that you can't refuse.

***

Wherever you obtain your car loan, don't allow the lender to talk you into buying credit life or disability insurance. Neither is a good deal for you. They're just two more ways to increase the profit margin on your loan at your expense.

Credit life insurance is a high profit margin item for lenders and most will try hard to sell it to you. Typically, you'll be told that if you love your family, you should afford them this protection. Some won't give you the opportunity to decline. They'll just write it into the contract without mentioning it.

Credit life insurance is nothing more than a term policy designed to pay off your loan in the event of your premature death. **It protects the lender, not you.** It has always seemed to me that the lender is the one who should be paying for credit life insurance since the lender is the sole beneficiary of the policy.

Disability insurance sold as part of a loan contract is even more expensive than credit life insurance—and it's something else that you probably don't need. If you are employed, you may have disability insurance through your employer. If not, you have workmen's compensation and Social Security coverage.

If you're self-employed, I hope you have disability insurance already. If not, call your agent today and sign up. Disability insurance for self-employed people whose business depends on their personal services is a must.

In any event, don't buy credit life or disability insurance as part of a loan contract. If the lender attempts to convince you that such coverage is mandatory, walk away and find another lender. In most states, suggesting that the loan cannot be granted unless you sign up would be a violation of the law.

If you've fallen for the pitch and feel that credit life and disability insurance is necessary in order to demonstrate your love for your family, and then buy it through your insurance agent. I'll guarantee you that it will cost you less.

***

If you must borrow, how much can you afford to go on the hook for?

There are any number of rules of thumb designed to help you decide how much money you can afford to borrow. I've seen some that factor in all sorts of esoteric variables and appear to reflect great scientific exactitude. Frankly, I don't think any of them are worth the parchment they're written on. If you want to avoid playing the sucker, decide now to stick to the next principle of sound money management:

- **Never borrow money unless you have no other choice. If you have no other choice, borrow as little as possible and shop for the best deal.**

So, how much is more than you can afford to borrow? If you can't figure out when you are overextending your ability to repay, this book isn't going to help you, nor will any other. Go back and read this chapter again.

CHAPTER SEVEN

The Tax Man Cometh

Our Constitution is in actual operation; everything appears to promise that it will last; but in this world nothing is certain but death and taxes.

—Benjamin Franklin (1706-1790)

In today's world, it's not what you earn that matters, it's what you keep after Uncle Sam has carved out his share. Life, alas, is a constant tug-of-war between you and the tax man. Too often, it's the tax man who manages to come out on top. But have heart. Regardless of what your barber tells you, it doesn't have to be that way.

Federal Judge Learned Hand summed up this point of view best. Many years ago, the famed jurist pointed out that while tax **evasion** is a crime, tax **avoidance** is not only legal, it's common sense. In other words, every person is entitled, even obligated, to pay as little in income taxes as the law will allow.

Unfortunately, our tax laws have become so absurdly complex that even the most seasoned professionals admit to confusion in trying to decipher their arcane passages. The most confused of all? The people who write our tax laws. If you don't think so, just show your congressional representative a paragraph of current tax law and ask him or her to explain it to you.

But one thing about taxes is abundantly clear: Every dollar that you don't pay in taxes is a dollar that can be used to enhance your lifestyle instead of being swallowed up in the bottomless maw of the U.S. Treasury.

Our income tax laws have given birth to a new way to describe our money. Before the first income tax laws were passed, we had just plain dollars to deal with. Today, we have before-tax dollars and after-tax dollars. It's extremely important that you understand the difference and how that difference can affect your life.

In the earliest days of the federal income tax, it was pegged at 1%. Back then, the difference in before-tax and after-tax dollars was relatively unimportant. Today, the difference is profound. With federal tax rates as high as 39.6%, the importance of protecting and increasing your after-tax dollars cannot be overestimated. And the gap between before-tax and after-tax dollars is almost certain to widen in the years to come.

Before-tax dollars are the dollars you earn at your job or through your investments. After-tax dollars are the dollars you have left after Uncle Sam has taken his bite out of your earnings.

By definition, then, $100 of after-tax money is worth much more to you than $100 of before-tax money. How much more will depend on your tax rate and whether you pay state or local income taxes as well as federal. If your total tax bite is, say, 33%, then $100 of before tax earnings is actually worth only $67 to you. But $100 in after-tax money is a full $100 that you can spend or put to work in your investment portfolio.

Using the above example of a total federal, state and local tax bite of 33%, you would have to earn 150 before-tax dollars in order to wind up with 100 after-tax dollars in your pocket.

So remember, the after-tax (or tax-free) dollars, that I speak of throughout this book are much more valuable to you than before-tax dollars, thanks to Uncle Sam.

***

Another important tax consideration that must not be allowed to escape your attention is what are called tax brackets. If you are to do a profitable job in tax avoidance, it is essential that you know which tax bracket you are in. Equally important, you must understand how tax brackets work.

Let's say that you earned $60,000 last year and paid $6,000 in federal income taxes. What tax bracket would you say you are in?

If you said 10%, please pay close attention.

Your tax bracket is actually much higher than 10%. But don't feel bad. Most people would have said the same thing. While it's true that you paid an **average** of 10% on your entire earnings, that's not what's important in tax matters. What is important is your marginal tax rate, not your average tax rate.

In America, we have what is called a graduated income tax. It means that you pay no income tax at all on the first few dollars you earn, and a high rate of tax on the last few dollars you earn. Theoretically, this means that the people with the highest incomes will pay a higher average tax rate than those with lower incomes. It doesn't always work out that way, but that's another story.

An easy way for you to see what tax bracket you are in is to dig out last year's tax records and the tax table in the instruction booklet you receive from the IRS each year. Now, add $1,000 to your taxable income and re-figure your tax from the tax table. The difference between the tax you actually paid and the tax you would have paid with another $1,000 in income will tell you what federal income tax bracket you're in.

Using the 1999 tax tables and assuming that you are a single person, your tax bill would be increased by $280 for a total of $6,280 on taxable income of $61,000. That figures out to an **average** tax rate of 10.3%, even though your true **marginal** tax rate is 28%. Put another way, 28% of every additional dollar of income you earn will go to the government in taxes, but only until you reach the next earnings plateau shown in the tax tables. At that point your marginal tax rate will go even higher.

FEDERAL
TAX BRACKETS AS OF THE YEAR 1999

	Taxable Income	Tax Bracket %
Single	$0—$25,750	15.0%
Joint	$0—$43,050	15.0%
Single	$25,751—$62,450	28.0%
Joint	$43,051—$104,050	28.0%
Single	$62,451—$130,250	31.0%
Joint	$104,051—$158,550	31.0%
Single	$130,251—$283,150	36.0%
Joint	$158,551—$283,150	36.0%
Single	$283,151	39.6%
Joint	$283,151	39.6%

Figure 2

Speaking of true tax rates, we aren't finished yet. To that 28% you must add another 7.65% for Social Security tax, bringing your true tax rate to 36.65%. That's $366.50 on $1,000 of earnings.

Does your state or local community, or both, have an income tax? If they do, you must add those taxes to get your true tax rate. As you can see, a total marginal tax rate of 40% is not at all unusual even for tax-payers of modest means.

Think about that. At a 40% tax rate, those time-and-a-half dollars you earn from working overtime may not be worth much more than your straight time dollars, and that extra $1,000 you earned from your part-time job netted you only $600.

That's why it is critically important for you to develop a basic understanding of our tax structure? It's absolutely essential that you do so if you are to maximize your after-tax dollars as you travel the road to financial independence? All of which brings us to the next principle of sound money management:

- **Every dollar that you avoid spending on taxes is a tax-free dollar, the most valuable kind. Therefore, you must do everything possible to keep your tax bill as low as possible.**

If you are to avoid taxes wherever possible, You need a solid understanding of the basics of our income tax and the workings of tax brackets. But you mustn't become consumed with the subject to the point where you lose perspective. In that regard, I will always remember a working associate of mine many years ago. Let's call him Jim. Jim hated paying income taxes. He especially hated the graduated tax structure because it increased his tax bill as his income went up.

Jim and I worked for a large company back then and most of us employees were delighted to learn that the company had granted an across-the-board wage increase.

Most of us, but not Jim. Jim was outraged. "That extra money just pushes me into the next tax bracket," he announced. "I figured it out last night. I'm going to wind up with less money in my pay envelope because my tax rate is going up."

Jim proclaimed that he was going to demand that the company cancel his raise because of this outrageous tax situation.

It took his friends a long time to convince Jim that although the number of tax dollars he would have to pay would go up as a result of his raise, so would his net pay. There is, of course, no way that being pushed into the next graduated tax bracket as a result of an increase in income can lower your after-tax income.

When Jim got his first paycheck after his raise, he saw for himself that his net pay had increased. Still, he continued to fume about the increase in his tax. Now that's dedication to a cause.

***

Keeping abreast of tax provisions as they affect you is a lifetime job. Even if you have a professional doing your taxes, keeping yourself knowledgeable on tax considerations that affect your situation is the best way to follow Judge Hand's advice. No one else, not even your brother-in-law's accountant, can be expected to keep a lid on your tax bill without a lot of help from you.

Considering the complexity and ever-changing nature of our tax laws, it's not possible to provide a comprehensive listing of every tax saving technique in a book such as this. It would be out of date before it could be printed. But here are enough solid ideas to demonstrate some of the many ways you can take the initiative in your war with the tax man.

Basically, there are three methods you can use to lower your tax bill and thus increase your stash of those all-important after-tax dollars: eliminate taxes, reduce taxes, and postpone taxes. All of the techniques that follow fall into one or more of these three categories.

If you're like me, the most attractive of the three techniques is "eliminating taxes." After all, why pay any tax if you can just eliminate taxes?

Sorry. Most of us will never be able to eliminate taxes entirely, but we can eliminate some taxes. One example of this technique is the purchasing of tax-free municipal bonds. If you are in the 31% or higher tax bracket, you can probably benefit by investing part of your portfolio in high-grade municipals. Savvy investors look for municipals issued in their home states. These are usually free of federal, state and local taxes. Thus, they are known as triple tax-frees in the industry.

The dollars paid to you in interest from tax-free bonds, particularly triple tax-frees, are after-tax dollars. Every one of those dollars goes directly into your pocket, or into your wealth-building portfolio, where they can generate still more dollars.

For many people, the sheer psychological triumph of generating income that is totally shielded from taxes is one of life's more satisfying experiences. Frankly, I can think of one or two activities that are more thrilling for me. Still, avoiding taxes does rank high on my list of passions.

If you are fortunate enough to have already built up a comfortable portfolio through savvy investing, there is yet another way to eliminate taxes entirely.

Let's say that you bought 100 shares of stock a few years ago for $1,000, and now that stock is worth $5,000. Let's also say that you plan to make a generous $5,000 contribution to you favorite charitable organization. You could write the charity a check for $5,000. If you do that, the charity will get $5,000 and you will get a $5,000 deduction on your taxes. If you're in the 31% bracket, that $5,000 donation will save you $1,550 in federal taxes.

But there's a better way:

You can donate the stock itself to the charity. The charity still gets the same $5,000 because it doesn't have to pay tax on the profit when it sells the stock. And you still get that $5,000 tax-saving deduction. But you get something extra. You avoid the capital gains tax on the $4,000 profit that you'd owe if you sold your shares yourself. That handy little tax avoidance maneuver saves you an extra $800.

As a bonus, the charity gets the benefit of the full market value of your donation. Since the charity is tax-exempt, they can sell the stock and pay no taxes.

Everyone except Uncle Sam wins in the above transaction, which is perfectly legal in every way. And you have the satisfaction of putting not one but two tax saving techniques to work. You've both reduced and eliminated taxes in the same transaction.

If you are in a position to make substantial donations to charity, you should consider donating appreciated stock or mutual fund shares instead of cash. This works even if you like the shares involved and don't want to give them away. Donate them anyway and then buy the same shares back on the open market with the cash you would have donated. Now you have your shares back, have benefited from the tax savings and you'll pay capital gains tax only on future appreciation of your shares.

Although this is a favorite tax-saving technique for wealthy taxpayers, you don't have to be wealthy to benefit from it. Your tax advisor or the charity you want to help should be able to work out the details for you.

***

Another way to reduce your overall tax burden is to save money in the names of your children. This neat little trick was made possible by the 1956 Uniform Gifts to Minors Act (UGMA). Later, when it became clear that a more flexible law was needed, the Uniform Law Commissioners adopted the Uniform Transfers to Minors Act (UTMA) in 1986. The primary focus of these laws was to provide a convenient way to make gifts of money and securities to minors. The end effect is an opportunity for you to save on your tax bill.

To take advantage of UTMA, open up a savings or brokerage custodial account in the name and Social Security number of your child or children. Under current law, children under 14 with no other income, will owe no tax at all on the first $700 of income from the account, with 15% tax due on the next $700. That makes a total of $105 in taxes due on the first $1400 of income. Compare that with your tax rate. If you were in the 39% tax bracket, you'd pay $546 on $1400 in income. That's a nice little savings of $441 in family taxes.

To be sure, the potential reduction in taxes through the use of a custodial account may seem relatively minor. However, if the donations you make to such an account are in line with your overall gift plans for the child, why not take advantage of whatever savings are possible?

Income in custodial accounts is taxed at the child's tax rate (which presumably is lower than yours). So, whatever money you place in your childrens' accounts will normally grow at a faster rate than it would in your own accounts where your own marginal tax rate would apply.

Custodial accounts are often used to build college funds for children. However, there are some disadvantages in using these accounts strictly for that purpose.

Current law allows you to give, free of gift tax, up to $10,000 per year to any individual, including your children. Your spouse may give an equal amount, for a maximum of $20,000 to any individual. These donations may be made to a custodial account. Of course, unless you are already wealthy, you can't afford to toss that much money around.

Even if you can afford to make large annual donations to a custodial account, it's not always a good idea, especially if you plan to apply for college tuition financial aid.

Remember, money in a child's name legally belongs to the child. When it's time to calculate how much financial aid a student can receive, colleges use a standard formula that penalizes families who have put savings in their child's name. Each school year, colleges normally require that children contribute about 35% of their own assets toward tuition, versus about 5.6% from the parents' assets. Of course, if you don't expect to apply for financial aid for tuition, this provision needn't concern you.

None of this is to suggest that custodial accounts are not practical for college funds. If you intend to make relatively small donations for a child's eventual use, for college or any other purpose, a custodial account may be the way to go. They are far easier and cheaper to set up than trusts or other alternatives.

However, if you plan to make large annual donations up to the maximum tax-free donation of $10,000, a Roth IRA account or a trust will usually be a better choice. Trusts are similar to custodial accounts, but they differ in some important ways.

***

Generally speaking, trusts are more expensive, complicated and time-consuming than custodial accounts. However, trusts provide greater protections and more flexibility. And, when properly constructed, trusts offer more potential tax savings than custodial accounts. You should definitely consider setting up a trust if you expect to transfer thousands of dollars into accounts for your children every year. Custodial accounts are more suitable for smaller transfers.

Trusts vs. Custodial accounts is a complex issue that varies considerably with individual circumstances. You should consult your attorney or tax advisor if you need advice on this matter.

In any case, remember that once you open any form of custodial account, you will no longer own the money you place in it. Once you transfer it, you can't take it back. That's why you should never transfer money into a custodial account if you have any concern that you might need it later for your own use.

As long as you plan to spend any withdrawals on the child, and as long as you do not ever expect to need the money for yourself, this is not a concern. As custodian, you will always be able to withdraw money from the account, provided it is to be spent on the child's behalf. Be careful here, though. Interpretations as to what qualifies as an expenditure directly benefiting the child can get problematic. The IRS keeps a close eye on this sort of thing and hassles with them on this issue are not uncommon.

When the child reaches age 21 (18 in some states), if there is any money left, you are required by law to relinquish custodianship. I should mention here that the so-called uniform laws resulting from UGMA and UGMA are anything but uniform. The National

Conference of Commissioners on Uniform State Laws proposes them. Then it's up to the individual states to determine whether they'll adopt them and what changes they'll make. If two states adopt the same uniform law, you can expect to see similar, but not necessarily identical, laws in those two states.

What all this means is that statements that are true about a uniform act are not necessarily true about the law in your state. Before you rely on anything you read here, check the law of your state.

At whatever point you are required to relinquish custodianship, you are out of the picture. The child has complete ownership of the account. You may relinquish control sooner if you like, but unless you do, the child does not have legal access until the age stipulated by the law in your state.

Despite all the cautions, custodial accounts can be a practical way to reduce your overall family tax bill. As long as you are aware of the limitations, you should keep the custodial account as one of your options.

If your estate is large enough for you to be concerned about estate taxes, you should avoid naming yourself as custodian. Ironically, if you die before a custodial account has been relinquished, the account will be included in your estate. The reasoning here, whether it makes sense or not, is that you retained the power to decide how your gift will be applied for the benefit of your child. You can avoid this problem by naming as custodian someone who will not make any gifts to the account. This might be a relative or a trusted close friend.

***

If you itemize deductions on your tax return, you should make yourself familiar with the list in figure 3. It shows a few of the deductions most often overlooked by itemizers.

Here's a reminder of some deductions you can easily overlook when you prepare your tax return. It is not intended to be all-inclusive nor applicable to everyone.

Accounting fees for tax preparation services and IRS audits

Alcoholism and drug abuse treatment.

Amortization of premium on taxable bonds.

Appraisal fees for charitable donations or casualty losses

Appreciation on property donated to a charity.

Casualty or theft losses.

Commissions and closing costs on sale of property.

Contact lenses, eye glasses, and hearing devices.

Contraceptives, if bought with a prescription.

Costs associated with looking for a new job in your present occupation

Depreciation of home computers.

Dues to labor unions.

Employee contributions to a state disability fund.

Employee's moving expenses.

Fees for a safe deposit box to hold investments (e.g., stock certificate).

Fees paid for childbirth preparation classes if instruction related to obstetrical care.

Foreign taxes paid.

Foster child-care expenditures.

Gambling losses to the extent of gambling gains.

Hospital services fees (laboratory work, therapy, nursing services, and surgery.

Impairment-related work expenses for a disabled individual.
Investment advisory fees.
IRA trustee's administrative fees billed separately.
Lead paint removal.
Legal abortion expenses.
Legal fees incurred in connection with obtaining or collecting alimony.
Margin account interest expense.
Medical transportation, including lodging
Mortgage prepayment penalties and late fees.
Out of pocket expenses relating to charitable activities
Part of health insurance premiums if self-employed.
Penalty on early withdrawal of savings.
Points on a home mortgage and certain refinancings.
Protective clothing required at work. .
50% of self-employment tax.
Seller-paid points on the purchase of a home.
Special equipment for the disabled.
State personal property taxes on cars and boats.
Subscriptions to professional journals.
Theft or embezzlement losses.
Trade or business tools with life of one year or less.
Worthless stock or securities.

Figure 3

One method for reducing taxes available to almost every taxpayer involves just a little juggling...of time, that is.

Shifting income and deductions between tax years is a popular technique for deferring and sometimes reducing taxes. Whenever possible, postponing your taxes until a later year is a profitable move. It allows you, rather than Uncle Sam, to have the use of the money involved.

In general, it makes sense to defer income until next year whenever you can, and accelerate deductions into this year whenever you can.

Accelerating deductions is easy. Just make as many payments as possible before the end of the year. Even if you make a few payments a little earlier than required, getting them into this year's deductions will help to decrease this year's taxes.

Deferring income can be a bit more complicated because of what the IRS calls constructive receipt. This refers to amounts of money that were available to you before the end of the year, even if you didn't actually take possession of the money until after the end of the year. Whenever it's possible though, deferring payments due you until next year while accelerating deductions into this year will often produce a tidy little tax savings.

***

A word of caution on tax avoidance: It can be carried to foolish, counterproductive extremes. Some people are so incensed at the idea of paying income taxes that they involve themselves in investment manipulations that are clearly self-defeating. Going to the extreme in trying to avoid paying income taxes can result in you winding up with fewer after-tax dollars than you would have if you ignored the subject entirely.

Take for example, a person in the 15% income tax bracket who insists on investing only in tax-free bonds because she detests the idea of paying income taxes. Because taxable bonds pay substantially more than municipals, people in the lower tax brackets will actually generate more after-tax dollars with taxable bonds than they would with the lower-paying municipals. As the bible admonishes, moderation in all things. Tax avoidance is no exception.

While tax considerations are always present in any investment decision, you must be careful to choose your investments first on the basis of their quality as investments. Never allow yourself to get hooked on a lousy investment just because it appears to be tax-sheltered. What good has it done you to work up a tax-sheltered deal if you lose all the money you've invested in it?

Which brings up the subject of those great tax shelters you've been hearing about? You know, the ones that wealthy investors have used to avoid paying income taxes. These are the complex deals that purport to make use of little-known tax loopholes. Put together by speculators, many of these deals have wound up causing nothing but grief for the suckers who bought into them. High promotional and administrative costs in even the most honest of these deals have often made them worthless, or worse than worthless, to the people who invested in them. In many cases, the IRS has declared them to be illegal tax evasion schemes, bringing more than a little grief to investors caught up in the swindle.

You probably won't be hearing as much about tax shelters these days. That craze reached its zenith in the 1980s. In those days, brokerage firms were paying their salespeople as much as 10 to 12% of the money they brought in from investors in tax shelters. The firms and many of their salespeople got rich while most of the investors took an unwanted bath.

The Tax Reform Act of 1986 sharply limited the types of tax-shelter schemes that can pass tax law muster. Yes, there are legitimate tax shelters around, some of which are sponsored by the government itself. Still, unless you are an extraordinarily sophisticated investor with extensive knowledge of legal and tax implications, you will do well to turn a deaf ear to the peddlers of tax shelters.

The spectacular exceptions to this rule are the tax-sheltered retirement programs designed and authorized by the federal government. We'll be talking about them in detail in a later chapter.

***

What about your home as a tax shelter?

In our society, the benefits of owning your own home are legion. That's why, if you do not already own your own home, it's so important to set home ownership as one of your top priorities. In addition to the homeowners' benefits discussed elsewhere in this book, you can add tax sheltering to the list.

First, any increases in the value of your home are not subject to taxes until you sell. With recent changes in the law, the first $250,000 of price appreciation is fully shielded from taxes when you sell your primary residence after age 55. For all but the wealthiest people living in the most expensive homes, that one-time exemption is going to mean that all of the price appreciation during their time of ownership is completely sheltered from taxes.

Not to be forgotten: The interest costs when paying down your home mortgage are tax-deductible, further enhancing home ownership as a wealth-building device.

***

Finally, what about the most effective tax elimination method of all: hiding your income from the tax man? After all, if you don't report some or all of your income, you won't owe any taxes on it. Right? What could be more effective than that?

Well, for one thing, flinging yourself in front of a Greyhound bus.

Uncle Sam may get a bit testy when you take questionable deductions on your tax forms, or when you use dubious maneuvers to minimize your taxes. But make no mistake, he gets downright hostile when you fail to report income (otherwise known as tax evasion). Hiding income from the tax man is a felony; you can go to jail for that unseemly conduct.

If you ever get tempted, you may want to read up on the history of America's most notorious gangster, Al Capone. The Feds couldn't prove any of the murders they were sure he committed, or any of the racketeering that the whole world knew he invented. All attempts to nail Capone for the hundreds of vicious crimes he was suspected of committing were for naught.

So how did they finally hang a rap on him that sent him to the penitentiary? You guessed it. Al Capone went to jail for income tax evasion.

Enough said?

If you still don't get it, go back to the beginning of this chapter and read the second paragraph again. Now you get it, don't you?

Judge Hand, are you listening?

Chapter Eight

Cover Your Assets

I advise you to go on living solely to enrage those who are paying your annuities. It is the only pleasure I have left.
—Voltaire (1694–1778)

In order to deal effectively with insurance companies, you must have a clear idea of exactly what this thing we call insurance is…and what it is not.

In its most basic definition, insurance is simply a contract between two parties: the insurer and the insured. The insurer is the insurance company and the insured is you, the customer.

The purpose of insurance is to provide compensation in the event of loss. Many kinds of insurance have been developed to cover a wide range of potential losses to the insured. As with most legal functions in America, all forms of modern insurance had their early beginnings in Great Britain.

No one knows when and to whom the first insurance policy was sold, but we do know a lot of how it evolved. The first form of insurance appeared in Britain in the 1500s. Then, as now, the British economy depended upon trading with other nations. Since Britain is an island, sailing ships were a critical necessity for world trade.

When a large ship loaded with goods for trade returned safely, considerable profit was made. However, if the ship did not return, the merchant lost everything and may well have faced financial ruin. In the face of these risks, groups of merchants got together and developed a master plan to reduce the risk of financial ruin should one of their ships be destroyed or lost at sea.

If a merchant lost a ship, the other merchants would each pay a specified amount of money to help compensate for his loss. While these payments would not fully cover the loss, they would at least provide enough money for the owner to continue in business. In return, if the voyage was successful, the merchant would give a percentage of his profits to the other merchants. Soon, sensing the profit potential in this arrangement, some merchants began putting together their own full-time insurance operations. Thus, the world's first marine insurance companies were born.

***

In America, the first insurance company to be formed was The Friendly Society, modeled after its English namesake, to insure houses and tenements. It had its beginning on January 18, 1732, in Charles Town (now Charleston) South Carolina. On that day the South Carolina Gazette announced the organization of The Friendly Society with a notice which read in part: "At a meeting of sundry of the Freeholder, of the Town at the House of Mr. Giguilliat, Proposals were offered for establishing an Insurance office against FIRE…"

Farther north in Philadelphia, Benjamin Franklin, in his Pennsylvania Gazette, was calling attention to the need for fire-fighting equipment in the City of Brotherly Love. Later, in its February 18, 1752 issue, the Gazette announced the formation of the second fire insurance company in America. On that day the articles of agreement, called "a deed of settlement," were signed establishing the Philadelphia Contributorship for the Insurance of Houses from Loss by Fire. This was a mutual company, incorporating a principle of which Franklin had already expressed approval: "whereby every man might help another without any disservice to himself."

Franklin's company was the first to make direct contributions toward fire prevention. It recognized certain fire hazards and either warned against them or simply refused to insure buildings where they existed. Wooden buildings, for example, were not accepted for insurance. Homeowners were cautioned not to smoke meat in their houses, a common practice at the time. They were permitted to have either shade trees or insurance, but not both. Trees were considered definite risks, attracting lightning and interfering with firemen's efforts to control fires. Of course, the insurance industry has evolved dramatically since then. Today, everyone in America, including you and me, is involved with and affected by the modern insurance industry in one way or another.

Health Insurance

If you're like me, a bit long of tooth, you remember the days when health insurance was inexpensive, hassle-free, and pretty much invisible. If you're too young to remember those days, you probably find it difficult to believe that such medical nirvana ever existed.

It did exist. And it wasn't all that long ago.

When the idea of prepaid health insurance was just catching on in the late 1940s and early 1950s, the premise was very simple: When you wanted to see a doctor, you went. Any doctor you chose would do just fine. Referrals were often given, but they were never required. You filled out the papers and the insurance company paid the doctor. All prescriptions were covered in full.

There were exclusions, of course. When you were in the hospital, the insurance wouldn't cover the cost of telephone service or a rental TV. There were others, too, but, for the most part, anything you expected to be covered was covered. I still remember the total bill I had to pay when my daughter was born in 1950. When it came time to check her and the baby out of the hospital, I had to fork over $3.50 for telephone rental.

But enough of this depressing nostalgia. Today, the cost of health insurance is rising astronomically, is loaded with endless hassles and copays, and is anything but invisible. It's something else, too. It's absolutely essential.

Arguably, there is no bigger risk of total financial ruin today than going without health insurance coverage. Almost overnight, a serious illness could find you broke and owing hundreds of thousands of dollars in unpaid medical bills. It happens every day. According to recent estimates there are an unbelievable 40 million Americans who do not have health insurance coverage. This is a major failure in our society and we must find some way to ensure that all Americans have ready access to proper medical care. Until that happens, you must do everything possible to make certain that you never become one of that unfortunate number.

The need for proper medical coverage is so urgent today that it isn't unusual for people to turn down excellent job offers with solid companies simply because of inferior medical insurance benefits. Conversely, I know of at least one young man who is remaining in a job well below his potential, solely because of the excellent medical coverage that it provides. With several small children, he is reluctant to risk a change of jobs and the possible loss or deterioration of his medical coverage.

So, your first job is to make certain that you find a way to get health insurance coverage. Your second job is to make sure that your coverage is giving you the protection you must have.

Because medical insurance offered by different employers, insurance companies and HMOs can vary widely, simply having coverage doesn't mean that you have adequate protection. It's up to you to examine your policy so that you can compare it with coverage offered by other policies. This step is too important to take for granted. Once you find that you are responsible for a huge bill not covered by your policy, it's too late to argue.

Life Insurance

Whatever you do, don't let anyone convince you that life insurance or insurance products are good investments.

Life insurance is insurance. That's all it is and that's all it should be. The various forms of life insurance policies often marketed as tax-advantaged investments may offer some tax advantages, but they are basically poor investments. At best, they do a mediocre job of the double-barreled responsibility of providing death benefits and a decent return as an investment.

Whole life insurance is often promoted as a form of forced savings, and the policy's cash value is touted as a handy source for a loan if you should need one. Let's face it, if you can't summon up the necessary self-discipline to "always pay yourself first," you'll do better to join a Christmas club at your local savings & loan. The cash value in a whole life policy can take years to build up to any meaningful value. Further, if you take out a loan against it, your death benefit will be reduced proportionately.

I know I'm not making any friends in the insurance industry here, but that's the way it is.

In a way, whole life insurance policies remind me of the toaster oven that my wife—for some unfathomable reason—seems to love. To me, that devilish device is neither a toaster nor an oven. It's both slow and inefficient in both departments. Much like the fabled jack-of-all-trades, it is clearly a master of none. In my pragmatic world, a toaster is a toaster and an oven is an oven. Any suggested relationship between the two is artificial and gimmicky. It's the same way with insurance.

Life insurance is insurance; investments are investments.

As with money and investments, insurance is a fact of life. We can't get away from it. In our society, attempting to function without the protective shield of certain types of insurance is imprudent, even dangerous. In most states, it's now illegal to drive without auto insurance. And, as I pointed out earlier, no one but a hopeless ninny would want to be without the protection of some form of medical insurance in today's world.

Since we have no choice but to live with our insurance salesperson, it's obviously prudent to make every effort to learn the inner workings of this arcane trade for ourselves. Like all good money managers, we want to make certain that we obtain the precise protection that we need without paying an unacceptably high price.

Many years ago, a man named Elmer Wheeler was dubbed as the world's greatest salesman—and he may well have been. Mr. Wheeler trained thousands of salesmen in his techniques and he often exhorted his pupils to "sell the sizzle, not the steak."

A steak, as he would point out, is just a piece of raw meat. But the aroma and the sizzle of a steak cooking on the grill and the mouth-watering taste are the real reasons why people buy a steak. Using a similar analogy, he would point out that a car is just a hunk of metal with wheels. What people are really looking for when they shop for a car are such things as status, comfort, and economy. These are the things that a skilled car salesman sells, not independent suspension or non-slip differentials. Even when selling cars, he admonished, always sell the sizzle, not the steak.

Nowhere were Mr. Wheeler's theories put into more enthusiastic practice than in the life insurance industry. With nothing more than intangibles to sell—not something that could be worn, touched, eaten or driven—insurance salesmen HAD to learn how to sell the sizzle, not the steak.

And learn they did.

With such raw emotions as love of family, fear of death, and concerns about money to play on, the insurance industry developed selling techniques of almost irresistible authority. It would be impossible to count the numbers of people who have bought expensive life insurance without having anything resembling a clear idea of what they had bought, why they bought it, and why it is so expensive.

Like banks, insurance companies are necessary components in our complex society. We need insurance. What we don't need are overpriced insurance products made to look like something other than what they are. You will always be paying for insurance. It's your job to try to make sure that you are not paying for something you don't need and don't want.

***

The astonishing complexity that permeates the life insurance industry makes it virtually impossible to do justice to its entire sweep in a single book chapter...or an entire book. In order for you and me to learn all that we really should know about how to buy insurance we would have to retreat to the mountain top, take up residence in a monk's cell and study for perhaps a year. Absent that kind of dedication, here are some of the most basic highlights that you really should take the time to read.

Of all the categories of insurance with which we must deal, life insurance is arguably the one that offers the most in opportunities to pay too much for products that you don't understand and didn't want.

In broad, simplistic terms, life insurance comes in two flavors: whole life and term life. In turn, whole life comes in three varieties: traditional, universal, and variable. For the most part, you should avoid any attempt to sell you a whole life insurance policy in any of its varieties. Whole life is the form of insurance that is supposed to offer a combination of investment value and death benefits.

As an investment vehicle, whole life insurance is a mediocre choice at best, downright lousy at worst. It is subject to the ravages of inflation and will not bring you the returns that you can find in most any other form of conventional investment. In short, don't buy into the idea that whole life insurance is a viable investment.

To be sure, there are some advantages to whole life. For one thing, the payments remain the same throughout your life, as compared to term insurance where annual rates go up as you age. In the long run, however, term insurance is a more cost-effective way to buy coverage.

Don't expect your insurance agent to agree with this. He may even disparage term insurance as a "cheap" substitute for "real" life insurance. Some agents will attempt to frighten prospects with stories about skyrocketing term insurance payments as the policyholder ages. Don't listen to any of these arguments. Your insurance agent will make more money off you if she sells you whole life insurance instead of term. That's the simple fact.

You, in turn, will make more money if you buy term insurance and invest the money you save while you are making those small payments required in the early years of term insurance. Follow the principles in this book and you will be financially healthy enough to drop your term insurance by the time you reach the age where the premiums get unwieldy.

One variation of term insurance that helps to minimize the disadvantage of gradually increased premiums as the insured ages is the guaranteed level premium policy. This type of policy guarantees to maintain the same premium level for a specified number of years. You may want to ask your insurance agent about it.

Recent legislation requires insurers to set aside more money to pay future benefits on term policies that guarantee to keep premiums level for more than 10 years. While this will probably work to the eventual benefit of policy holders, some companies are already raising prices or juggling the terms of the guarantee as they figure out how to compete under the new rules.

For basic death benefit protection, go out and buy yourself a simple term life insurance policy. In most cases, you'll save a lot of money and you'll have a simple policy that is easy to understand. Shopping for whole life insurance can be incredibly complicated; term insurance is relatively simple to buy. Your term policy won't be encumbered with any complicated "cash surrender value" provisions, and you'll have a dependable death benefit in the exact face amount shown on the policy. Just make sure that there is a guaranteed renewable clause in the policy and that you are protected against cancellation. That's as simple as it can get, and that's the way life insurance should be bought. Our next principle of sound money management says it all:

- **If you need to buy life insurance protection, tell your insurance agent that you want a term policy. Reject any form of whole life insurance.**

An independent agent can be invaluable in helping you to shop around for the best policy and the best insurance company for your needs. Still, like the card player who trusts everyone in the game but wants to cut the cards anyway, you should shop around a little on your own. The Wholesale Insurance Network (800-808-5810) will be happy to send you free price quotes and applications for term insurance from a number of insurance companies. Just give them a call and tell them what coverage you would like.

***

So, how much life insurance is enough?

The most important issue to clarify when deciding on the amount of life insurance to buy is why you are buying it. Life insurance on your life obviously provides no benefit to you. It is for the sole purpose of providing financial relief for those of your survivors who depend on you for their support. How many of these people there are and how much help they will need are the defining factors that determine how much insurance you should have.

If you are single and have no one depending on you, you don't need any life insurance at all, unless you want to buy a small policy to keep your mother from being stuck with your funeral expenses. On the other hand, if you have a wife and six children, they are going to suffer financially if you die and leave them without adequate coverage on your life.

The need for insurance coverage decreases sharply for most people, as they grow older. Once your children have grown and you have accumulated a sizeable estate, you may need no life insurance at all.

Obviously, then, the variations on this theme are almost infinite. That's why no simple table or rule of thumb can de depended on to tell you how much insurance to buy. You should consult with your insurance agent, accountant and trusted family members in making this important decision.

What about life insurance for your children?

Forget it. Unless your child is a movie star supporting you, don't waste your money.

Disability Insurance

Recently, the owner of a small landscaping business that takes care of our yard work asked me to help him with some business problems. He had plenty of time to spend with me since he had just broken his ankle playing a little one-on-one with his teen-aged son.

Like a lot of small-business owners, Tom has life insurance but no disability insurance. Since his own personal efforts are the nucleus of his business, this period of six weeks or so during which he wasn't able to work were very costly for him. If he follows my recommendation, he won't be caught in this fix again. No self-employed person should ever risk the dangers of uninsured disability.

Unlike life insurance, disability insurance is designed to protect you (and your family) from financial hardship while you are still alive. In my view, disability insurance is at least as important, if not more so, than life insurance for self-employed breadwinners. According to some reports, as many as one-third of all workers will eventually suffer a disability that keeps them out of work for at least 90 days.

Remember, it doesn't take an apocalyptic tragedy to put you out of work for a while. A broken leg or a minor auto accident can do the trick just fine.

If you are an employee, depending on your employer and the state in which you live, you probably have some protection against disability, perhaps all you need. You should familiarize yourself with exactly how much protection you have, though; it may be far less comprehensive than you think. Yes, I know that Social Security also offers disability coverage, but qualifying for the government's definition of "disabled" has turned out to be a lot tougher than many people expected it to be.

When you go out to buy a disability policy, please don't hesitate to shop around. Insurance contracts are full of the most arcane language that you can imagine, written deliberately, I believe, to make it difficult for you and me to understand. If you are lucky enough to have an insurance agent in whom you have full trust, you'll need his help. This is an excellent illustration of why it is better to work with a trustworthy independent agent who is not tied to a single insurer.

Even with a good agent and a batch of price quotes, you need to be informed well enough to understand your basic needs. As with life insurance, you want to make sure that your policy is guaranteed to be both renewable and noncancelable so long as you pay your premiums on time. Your policy should also allow you to purchase additional coverage as your income grows and your needs change. Perhaps most important, it must contain coverage for a long-term disability, guaranteeing your payments at least until the normal retirement age of 65. It is here that an inflation provision is essential. If you suffer a long-term disability, the value of your payments will erode over time unless your policy contains a provision to adjust payments for inflation.

How much disability should you buy? As with life insurance, that all depends on your needs. As a rule of thumb, some insurance advisors suggest that coverage amounting to 70 to 75% of your current income is about right. Disability insurance payments are non-taxable, so you won't need 100% of your normal income to maintain your standard of living.

Auto Insurance

Have you been griping lately about the high cost of your auto insurance? O.K., let's take out that dusty old policy and take a look at it. No, you don't have to plod through all that impossibly small print. Just find the big print, the print that tells you about your collision deductible.

Does it say $50? Wow, that's great. That means that your insurance company will pay all but the first $50 to repair your car if you have an accident. Very comforting. But consider this:

Your insurance company is very pleased to offer you this arrangement because it knows a couple of things you may not know. To begin with, most forms of auto insurance are very profitable, and the more insurance you buy, the more profit the insurance company makes. That's why you should go into the insurance business yourself by self-insuring for small accidents.

If you call up your insurance agent and ask him how much less it would cost you if you raised that deductible to, say, $250, you'll find out how profitable the business can be. My guess is that you'll save a minimum of $150 per year by going to a $250 deductible, and, like all money that you save by not spending, that $150 is tax-free money. If you're in the 29% tax bracket, you have to earn $212 in order to wind up with $150 in your pocket. If you're in a higher tax bracket or if you pay local or state income taxes, raise that figure accordingly. Unless you're accident prone, that $150 will be yours year after year and will soon add up to important savings.

Yes, it's true, if you do have an accident, you'll pay the first $250 instead of $50. But that's what insurance is all about. Another thing that insurance companies know that you may not know is that many people never report small accidents because they fear that the insurance company will raise their rates (and they're right). So, they wind up paying for repairs on small claims themselves.

How much sense does that make? Why pay for that low-end coverage if it's unlikely that you're going to use it?

And remember, if you do have to pay part of the cost for collision repairs, that's a deductible expense on your tax return. So, Uncle Sam would assume part of your cost as a casualty loss. If you can afford to take the risk of paying for minor repairs, why pay a profit to someone else to take the risk for you? Take the risk yourself and invest those after-tax dollars.

I did the arithmetic years ago and decided to raise my own collision deductible to $500. As a result, I've pocketed thousands of after-tax dollars over the years. You can do the same if you're willing to assume the risk of the first $250 or $500 dollars for collision repairs. Don't forget, the money you save using this technique should be invested in your portfolio to help speed you on your way to financial independence. No fair taking it to Atlantic City.

By the way, this money-saving principle works precisely the same way on your homeowner's insurance. Maybe you ought to dig out that policy as well and take a look at the deductible. I can hear you now laughing all the way to the bank.

As is the case with all insurance, you should shop around when you are ready to buy or renew auto or home insurance of any kind. If you don't know where to start, log on to the Internet at www.quotesmith.com. They'll give you instant quotes on life as well as auto and medical insurance. You get quotes from a variety of companies and you choose the company to buy from. This site also segregates guaranteed from nonguaranteed term policies.

Another good site for instant quotes from a number of companies is www.insweb.com. If you like the idea of speaking directly with an agent, try www.accuquote.com. Leave your phone number and an agent will follow up.

Or use your telephone for quick quotes. Call GEICO (800-841-3000. They'll give you a quote right over the phone. Even if you're not ready to buy, these are great ways to compare your present cost with what else is available.

Annuities

There is one form of instrument offered for sale by insurance companies that does not pretend to do double-duty. They are called annuities and are sold as tax-deferred investment vehicles for payout beginning at retirement. Frankly, I can see no good reason to buy any form of annuity.

While it's true that your investment grows tax-deferred in either a fixed or variable annuity, it is fully taxed as ordinary income when you withdraw it. That's true with IRA and Keogh retirement accounts (discussed later) as well, but you get no tax deduction when you make your initial deposit in an annuity.

If you're looking for income, tax-free municipals offer a more hassle-free investment with no tax due, ever. If you want the best tax-deferred vehicle for retirement, an IRA or Keogh account is a better bet.

Insurance you don't need.

Life insurance on the kids isn't the only kind of insurance that you don't need. Flight insurance sold at airports is probably one of the worst investments you can make. Air travel is a remarkably safe form of transportation. Statistics have shown the risk of death on an ordinary flight to be as low as 1 in 10 million. It's so seldom that a claim is placed against those policies that only about five cents out of each dollar of income goes to pay claims. The rest is marketing expense and profit.

How about cancer insurance? Some insurance consultants say that it never makes sense to insure against a single disease. Buy cancer insurance and you'll probably die from a stroke, or get run over by a Greyhound bus.

Cancer insurance salespeople point out that one out of three people in the U.S. will eventually get cancer. But that doesn't address the issue of coverage limitations common in cancer policies.

Remember, these policies pay only if you get cancer.

Even if you get cancer, some policies pay only for the time you are in the hospital. Today cancer treatment, including radiation, chemotherapy and some surgery, is often given on an outpatient basis, meaning there is no hospital stay. When there is a hospital stay for a cancer patient the average time is only 13 days. So, a policy that pays only when you are hospitalized is obviously of limited value.

Many cancer insurance policies have fixed dollar limits. For example, a policy might pay only up to $1,500 for surgery costs or $1,000 for radiation therapy, or it may have fixed payments such as $50 or $100 for each day in the hospital. Others limit total benefits to a fixed amount such as $5,000 or $10,000.

No policy will cover cancer diagnosed before you applied for the policy. Some policies will deny coverage if you are later found to have had cancer at the time of purchase, even if you didn't know you had it.

When it comes to the possibility of getting cancer, or any other serious disease, your best bet is to make certain that you have solid overall health insurance coverage.

Still, if you feel strongly that you are at risk for cancer and prefer to buy a cancer policy despite the limitations, the peace of mind it offers may be worth it to you. If you do decide to buy such a policy, it is very important that you shop around carefully. Variations in price and coverage for cancer insurance are huge and confusing.

Credit life insurance, insurance on rented cars and "appliance insurance," all covered elsewhere in this book, are other forms of insurance that are simply bad buys.

***

Can you learn more about insurance on the Internet?

Of course you can. You can learn more about **anything** on the Internet. Not only can you find helpful general information on insurance there, shopping the Internet is also becoming a very smart way to buy insurance. There are any number of sites available, some of which enable you to get immediate quotes.

To find an appropriate insurance web site, log on to one of the major search engines. I like "All the Web All the Time." You'll find it at http://www.ussc.alltheweb.com. Click on "exact phrase," then type in what you are looking for, e.g. "Credit life insurance." You'll wind up knowing more than you ever wanted to know about the subject.

Some sites, as you might imagine, belong to the insurance companies themselves. Personally, I avoid those because of the obvious need for the companies to present the subject from their own perspective. While there is nothing improper about that, it hardly makes for objective counsel. Kind of like asking your plumber to come over and check out your house to see if anything needs attention.

One of the most informative, objective and easy to navigate insurance sites that I've found is: www.quicken.com/insurance. Check it out.

Whether you look to the Internet or to conventional sources to help with your insurance decisions, please remember that insurance company representatives are, by any definition, salesmen. While there is nothing wrong in consulting with a knowledgeable salesman in any field, it's up to you to maintain your perspective. Even the kindest, most sincere, and most knowledgeable salesperson doesn't make any money unless she sells you something.

Human nature being what it is, you would be wise indeed to never lose sight of that fact

CHAPTER NINE

What Rules?

Money changes all the iron rules into rubber bands.
—Ryszard Kapuscinski (b–1932)

Let me tell you straight out: This is my favorite chapter. No, it isn't because it's the shortest chapter in the book; it's for a different reason entirely. If I have come to relish one part of my fiscal education over all others, it was the discovery that there are no rules.

Now don't get me wrong. I'm not talking about the rules that most of us try to live by—the Golden Rule, not breaking in line at the supermarket, coming to a full stop at stop signs, and the like. Those rules, like the Marquis of Queensbury rules, hold potential benefits for all the participants.

Actually, I'm all for rules. In fact, I'm a rule aficionado if there ever was one. After all, we couldn't drive our cars, play a round of golf, or vote on election day if we didn't have rules to guide us. The rules that I say don't exist (or shouldn't exist) are the self-serving rules imposed by organizations and individuals that benefit no one except the people who attempt to impose them on others.

Those kinds of "rules" manage to survive because of the large number of us who are intimidated when we hear such admonishments as, "You can't do that, it's against our rules." If you're one of those people who slinks away with your tail between your legs when you hear such scoldings, even when you have a good case, read on and suffer no more.

My own addiction to rule-breaking started harmlessly enough. Miss Thomas, my junior high school English teacher of many years ago was a stickler for rules. According to Miss Thomas, all manner of unseemly things would happen to anyone foolish enough to break the stern rules of grammar by which she lived. To split an infinitive or to end a sentence with a preposition was, to Miss Thomas, roughly akin to defaming one's mother.

I wasn't brave enough to incur Miss Thomas's wrath by breaking any of her rules when I was writing something that she might see. But, in my secret writings I began to joyously split infinitives and write incomplete sentences that lacked either a subject or a predicate. Like this. Soon I began searching for good prepositions to end sentences with. What a rush. I was hooked on breaking rules for life.

From the relative boredom of breaking rules of grammar, I soon graduated to the exciting world of serious rule-breaking.

Let me give you a few examples of the kind of "rules" that I'm talking about—rules that you shouldn't pay the slightest bit of attention to; indeed, shouldn't even acknowledge. I daresay that once you get the hang of it, you'll enjoy ignoring (and breaking) those rules as much as I do.

***

A few years ago, I was shopping in an upscale gift shop and was startled to hear the sound of glass crashing to the floor. A frisky young child had accidentally knocked a glass vase to the floor where it shattered in a thousand pieces. With the mother and the child both in tears, the store owner sternly pointed to a sign on the wall that said, "You break it, you own it."

"I'm sorry," he said to the distraught customer, "but you owe me $49.95."

With hands trembling and tears flowing, the woman pawed through her purse and finally came up with fifty dollars which she obediently handed to the store owner. I wanted to tell the woman to hold on to her money, but the entire affair was clearly none of my business.

While I could empathize with the store owner as well as feel sorry for the customer, the simple fact is that the woman was not obligated to pay anything. Accidents in a retail store are a part of the cost of doing business. Accidental breakage, if it isn't covered by insurance, is a legitimate tax deduction for the owner, but that's all.

Management can put up any sign that it chooses in its stores. And there is nothing to stop management from establishing a "rule" that shifts responsibility for accidents to the customer. But such a rule is meaningless. I asked two attorney friends about this and they both agreed. The courts would be unlikely to recognize such a rule. Even if they did, enforcing it would be an impractical matter. So, our next principle of sound money management is:

- **If you accidentally break a piece of merchandise while shopping in a retail store, remember that you have no obligation to pay for it.**

If you ever find yourself in that fix, I suggest that you offer your earnest apologies to store personnel while keeping your hand firmly fixed on your wallet.

But what if you are feeling pangs of conscience? Suppose you feel responsible for your graceless bumbling, feel sorry for the owner, and would like to ease your conscience. Fine. If you insist, go ahead. But ask the manager to show you written evidence of the **cost**, not the selling price of the ill-fated merchandise. To allow the store to generate a profit from your accident will permanently disqualify you from admittance to the Money Manager's Hall of Fame.

✳✳✳

Banks are more skilled than most organizations in crafting rules designed to intimidate the acquiescent. One of their favorites involves their handling of CD maturities. A few chapters back, you read about the time I allowed a bank to automatically renew a CD, something I have never done since. By the time I discovered the horrendously poor interest rate they applied to the renewal, the grace period had already expired.

According to the bank's rules, the customer service clerk told me, nothing could be done. The new CD was in effect and it couldn't be changed without an early withdrawal penalty.

You know the rest of that story. I persisted and finally spoke with a manager who never mentioned the "rule." Within minutes, the change was made and I wound up with a new interest rate almost 50% higher than the one I was given automatically.

Was I unreasonable in this matter? I think not. As a good customer of the bank in question, I made the mistake of putting my confidence in the bank. I reasonably assumed that I would be given the best available rate if I allowed my CD to renew automatically, a rate that any stranger walking in off the street could get. But, apparently, that's not the way the bank's rule-makers felt about such matters. The fact that the adjustment was made so quickly and with such ease left me thinking that I had caught the bank with its sticky fingers in my cookie jar.

***

Insurance companies are among the best creators of "rules." Unfortunately, most of their rules, even some of the worst of them, have been upheld through law and custom over the years. If an insurance company decides not to pay off your claim, there's a pretty strong chance that you will be the loser.

But that doesn't mean that you should let them get away with all of their "rules." Take the matter of your homeowner's insurance, for example.

Chances are the "limit of liability" on your homeowner's policy has been creeping up gradually over the years. That figure, the limit of liability, is what the company will pay you if your home burns to the ground. It is, they tell me, the estimated cost of completely rebuilding your home on the same piece of property. There would be no compensation for the land since, presumably, it would be undamaged by the fire. Since costs generally go up every year, regular increases in your limit of liability and your homeowner's premium would seem appropriate. That all seems logical enough, but let's take a closer look.

You won't find much, if any, information in your policy about just how limit of liability is computed (the companies use a more-or-less standard formula based on the physical configuration of your home). And I don't think you'll find any information at all on how they decide on the rate of increase each year (again, another formula). The result, I'm sorry to say, is a premium for your policy based on esoteric formulae to which you have no access.

An inquiry about all of this to your insurance agent may well bring you an answer similar to the one I got the first time I asked: "It's all done automatically based on the formulas. It works the same for everybody," they told me. I was left to understand that this was the way it worked and I could do nothing to change it.

They aroused my interest in all this again when my last premium notice arrived. There it was, another substantial increase in my limit of liability and, of course, in my premium. What troubled me was the amount of the limit of liability. This figure was considerably larger than my home would bring if I sold it. Further, if I sold it, the land would be part of the package, part of the price I'd get.

I told this to my agent. My home, I explained, simply isn't worth the amount of money that they apparently insure it for. He, in turn, explained to me that if my home burned to the ground, the company would pay me the full limit of liability, which would cover the cost of rebuilding the home on my existing property. That is more than it would cost to go out and buy an equivalent existing home, he explained.

All of this sounds quite logical on the surface. The bottom line, though, is that this arrangement can result in you insuring a piece of your property for much more than it's worth. Yes, the company will pay you the full limit of liability should your house burn down. But, meanwhile, you're paying higher premiums every year than you need to pay to replace your home if it's lost.

When I expressed my concern about all of this, my agent acknowledged that the rule could be bent. He revealed that he was permitted to adjust my limit of liability to the market value of my home right on the telephone. He did so and my premium was reduced on the spot by $80 per year.

Yes, yes, I know. If my home burns down, I'll only get fair market value for it. But as it happens, that's fine with me. The whole episode gives me even more motivation to keep my house from burning down, and I have eighty more after-tax dollars a year to play around with.

If this sounds OK with you too, and your home is insured for much higher than its fair market value, you may want to have a talk with your own insurance agent.

Keep in mind, though, that the burden for making sure that you are insured adequately rests with you. If you are more comfortable going with the figures compiled by your insurance company, by all means do so. At least you know the "rule" can be broken if you wish.

***

When it comes to drama, there is probably no better illustration of the "no-rules" premise than the case of Edward Petraiuolo, Jr. One day as Mr. Petraiuolo, 69, lay in a hospital room awaiting a lifesaving liver transplant, hospital personnel stopped by his room with some news: Medicare would not cover his surgery.

The reason: Medicare had passed a rule earlier that it would not cover liver transplants caused by hepatitis B virus.

Kay, Mr. Petraiuolo's wife turned out to be a rule-buster supreme. Desperate that her husband might not be able to get his transplant, she set out on what would have appeared on the surface to be an impossible mission: to get Medicare to pay for her husband's lifesaving transplant despite their "rule" against it. Not only did she wind up getting her husband a new liver all paid for by Medicare, her crusade resulted in a permanent change in Medicare's policy. Today, Medicare covers all hepatitis B victims needing liver transplants.

How did Mrs. Petraiuolo pull off this apparent miracle? It's a long and involved tale, but it involved extraordinary determination and not a small amount of sheer luck.

She began by questioning doctors, nurses and hospital officials about the reasoning behind the rule that could mean the death of her husband. She learned that the rule was originally passed because people who received liver transplants made necessary by hepatitis B did not fare as well as those whose transplants were made necessary by other causes.

She also found out that post-surgery results for those victims had improved dramatically since the rule had been passed. Still, the rule remained in place.

Armed with whatever knowledge she had been able to put together, Mrs. Petraiuolo contacted her U.S. representatives in Congress. As it turned out, both of the lawmakers were well known at the agency responsible for Medicare and they went to work to see what they could do.

A top official at the agency was informed about the case. He reviewed the facts and the latest data on liver transplant survivals by hepatitis B patients and made a major decision. In a rare if not unprecedented move, he directed that the agency must cover the expense of the transplant and the post-surgery drugs, despite the rule specifically prohibiting it

Did the official get into trouble for violating the rule? Apparently not. A short time later, an official announcement declaring that Medicare would henceforth cover liver transplants caused by hepatitis B was released.

How many people would have accepted the news that Mrs. Petraiuolo received that fateful day? How many people would have been resigned to the fact that a U.S. government agency had passed a rule denying coverage for a lifesaving operation? How many people would have said, "You can't fight city hall," and left in tears.

But not Kay Petraiuolo. Like you and me, she knows what we mean when we say, "There are no rules."

***

One of the newest "rules" that you need to break is the rule that some companies impose when you apply for credit.

Remember a while back, I told you that you must protect your Social Security number? That's because your life can be turned into a horrendous ordeal if you become the victim of the latest high-tech crime, stolen identity. That's when a scam artist obtains enough personal information about you to assume your identity. In short, that person becomes you.

That way, the perpetrator can destroy your credit by using your name to make credit purchases, can obtain driver's licenses and other legal documents in your name, can even commit crimes for which the police may come looking for YOU. And convincing them that you aren't the guilty one can be your worst nightmare come true.

What's the easiest way for a criminal to assume your identity? That's an easy question. The best way of all is to get his hands on your Social Security number.

That's why you should refuse to divulge your SS number to anyone except government agencies or banks (banks or any institution dealing with your money and required to make reports to the IRS are required to obtain your SS number).

Unfortunately, there are still a few major companies that are slow in getting the message. Giant Eagle supermarkets were requiring customers to give their SS numbers in order to obtain the company's shopper's card. Customer complaints were so vigorous that the company eventually dropped the policy. As of this writing, a national building supply company and a Pennsylvania cable TV company are embroiled in disputes with customers because of their insistence on getting SS numbers on their applications for credit. I'm sure there are many other similar cases around the country.

If you refuse to provide your SS number when you apply for credit and the credit application is turned down. Be sure to ask why the application was rejected. Federal law requires that credit providers must tell applicants the specific reason their credit was turned down.

There is no legitimate reason for credit providers or other organizations to require Social Security numbers before doing business with you. If you give in to it, the risk is all yours. That's the reason for our next principle of sound money management:

- **Never divulge your Social Security number to anyone except appropriate government agencies or banks. If a retailer or lender demands your SS number, find someplace else to do business.**

A great place for finding "rules" is in contracts. As I mentioned earlier, you should never sign any type of contract without first reading it carefully. And be sure to keep a special lookout for any contract that is offered to you as "our standard contract." Every time I'm asked to sign a contract described that way, I read it with special care.

What's that you say? You rarely get involved with signing contracts. Oh yes you do.

Just about everything you affix your signature to these days is a contract. Whether it's called a lease, an agreement, a proposal, a bill of sale, or any of dozens of other types of written instruments, it is a legal contract. Once you sign it, you are obligated to live up to its terms, even if you didn't understand what you were signing, and even if the terms are grossly unfair.

Once you get into the habit of reading contracts before you sign them, you'll find lots of provisions that you don't agree with...even ones that you find totally unacceptable. When you call attention to such clauses, you may be met with a reply that goes something like this: "That's our standard contract, we can't change anything in it."

Don't you believe it.

Whenever you are handed a contract to sign, the wording in that contract was carefully crafted to favor the creator of the contract. Count on it. Leases are a good example.

I've never seen a "standard" lease that didn't heavily favor the landlord. If you're a desirable potential tenant and the landlord wants your business, she'll agree to reasonable changes in the lease terms. The key word here is "reasonable." Most landlords clearly understand that the basic lease they offer to their tenants contains clauses that favor the landlord. If the potential landlord refuses to eliminate unreasonable clauses, you'd better find a new place to rent. Else you may find yourself tied up in a lease that will keep you awake nights.

Everything that applies to real estate leases goes double in automobile leases. Watch out especially for the amount of down payment, precisely what happens when the lease expires, and at what point you will be required to pay for excess mileage. The time to worry about these things is NOT after you get home and settle in your easy chair to read the lease.

Of course, your salesperson may imply that the lease is a "standard" form that everyone signs with no changes. Don't you believe it. While the lease you are considering may be a reasonable one with no objectionable clauses, don't take it for granted. Before you sign on the dotted line, take a copy home where you can read it at your leisure.

One friend who has leased cars for his business for years told me that he has never signed a lease without making at least one change in wording, or scratching out at least one phrase.

After trying it a few times myself, I'll have to admit that there is no more enjoyable time to break "rules" than when you are getting ready to sign a contract. Try it. You'll like it.

CHAPTER TEN

Important Decisions—Think Twice, Act Once

Shall I show you the muscular training of a philosopher? What muscles are those? A will undisappointed; evils avoided; powers daily exercised; careful resolutions; unerring decisions.

—Epictetus. Circa 60 A.D.

Life would be much easier if we weren't called on to make so many decisions. What tie should I wear today? Can I afford the extra calories from putting cream cheese on my bagel? Should I tell the boss about his secretary and the janitor? Should I watch NYPD Blue or go to the movies?

Those are the tough decisions, the ones that only you can make. Fortunately, most decisions involving personal money management can be noodled out with a little common sense, and maybe a little help from your friends. Here are a few of that type:

Should I sign up for a Service Contract on that new TV set I'm buying?
The next time you buy a major home appliance or a piece of electronic gear, you will almost certainly be asked to purchase something called a service contract, maintenance agreement, extended warranty, or some similar euphemism.

Don't.

These instruments are nothing more than a form of insurance masquerading under another name. The companies that sell service contracts don't want people calling them insurance because they don't want their products to come under the jurisdiction of state insurance agencies.

Whenever some state legislator comes up with a bill that would define service contracts as a form of insurance, the big guns in the industry line up in full battle gear to oppose the measure. One of their biggest weapons is the careful avoidance of using any name that suggests the concept of insurance. Thus, the parade of non-legal sounding names like maintenance agreement, service contract, extended warranty, etc.

It isn't that there's anything illegal, or even shady, about the idea of selling warranty protection. Many of America's most prestigious companies sell service contracts. And they do provide insurance (you should excuse the expression) against unexpected repair bills.

It's just that they are terribly overpriced. So much so, that the sale of service contracts often provides more profit to the retailer than the products themselves. The sale of service contracts is so important to some retailers and car dealers that their salesmen are constantly reminded that selling a high percentage of service contracts is a basic part of their job responsibility. In some companies, the pressure to sell service contracts has been so intense that salespersons have revolted by approaching unions or by filing complaints with the National Labor Relations Board.

Unless you happen to be of those star-crossed souls who are as intimately acquainted with the repairman as you are with your children, you'll save a lot of money by avoiding service contracts. It's true, that the sudden failure of a TV picture tube or washing machine timer can provide a financial jolt to the average household budget. But the economics over the long haul says that you will pay more money for repairs if you buy service contracts...probably a lot more.

***

Remember that the seller of service contracts has a huge advantage over you. He has years of records that tell him exactly how much revenue is brought in by the sale of contracts, and exactly how much money has been spent to honor them. Using that information, which no one else has, he can set up a pricing schedule that virtually guarantees a high profit margin. What other product can make that statement?

Another group that thrives on the sale of extended warranty contracts is America's new and used car dealers. While it is always important to read any contract **before** signing it. That goes double if you're thinking about signing up for a service contract on an automobile.

Never allow yourself to lose sight of the fact that you are buying only what the contract specifically says you are buying. If it isn't mentioned in black and white, it isn't covered.

Many auto contracts have a section titled "What this contract covers," or something similar. A really nice feature, it would seem—plain language telling you exactly what is covered. Keep in mind, though, that section was put in there to protect the dealer as much as to protect you. While it carefully outlines what **is** covered, it doesn't tell you what **is not** covered.

If you develop a leaky oil pan gasket and your contract doesn't specifically say that it covers leaky oil pan gaskets, you've been had.

If you insist on buying a service contract (extended warranty) on your automobile, ask to see, in writing, what is NOT covered by the contract. Tell your salesman that you want to take a copy of the contract home to read it over before you sign it. If he balks, you walk.

There are literally thousands of things that can go wrong with an automobile. Keep that in mind when you look over the section titled, "What This Agreement Covers."

My advice: The next time a salesman asks you to buy a service contract, ask how much it will cost. Then say no and put that amount of money into your investment portfolio instead. You will probably get hit with a big repair bill now and then. But, over the years, you'll be way ahead.

Should I lease my next car?

Absolutely not, unless you are in a business that will allow you to take the lease payments as a deductible business expense. Even then, you should lease only when the money you would use to buy your car could be put to work in your business at a higher rate of return than the cost of the lease.

Forget the seductive ads that imply a cost savings through leasing. That's pure fiction. "Leasing has all the headaches and responsibility of owning and none of the benefits," says Jack Gillis, a spokesperson for the Consumer Federation of America in Washington, D.C.

And forget the fact that so many people are falling for the leasing mystique. You're in for a lifetime of disappointments if you let yourself think that the public in general acts in a prudent fashion.

There's a reason why auto dealers promote leasing so heavily. It's very profitable. Flat out, a leased car is going to cost you more money—considerably more money—than you would pay to buy the same car. Most leasing contracts carry a difficult-to-uncover high interest rate. And when you lease, you are financing almost the entire cost of the car at that high interest rate. If you don't believe me, ask your accountant.

If you still insist on leasing your car, at least don't fall for the salesman's pitch to put as much money down as possible. While it's true that a larger down payment means lower interest cost when you are buying a car, that's not true when you are leasing, according to Mr. Gillis.

What is a good amount to put down? "Nothing," says Gillis. "The whole point is that the one benefit of leasing is that you don't have to put anything [or very little] down."

Which, by the way, is why many people opt for the lease; they don't have the money for a down payment. Putting a larger down payment on a lease will not proportionately reduce the monthly payments. So, our next principle is:

- **Never lease your personal car. Over time, you'll wind up paying new car prices, but you'll never own the car.**

Leasing may look attractive on the surface. And it certainly does make it possible for people who cannot come up with the down payment for a new car to drive a new car. In the end, though, those same people would be far better off buying and driving a used car.

What about those rebates offered on some new cars? Are they legitimate?

Sure, the rebates that are frequently offered on various models of new cars are legitimate. The money comes directly from the factory in a promotional effort to juice up sales. However, if you insist on using the dealer to finance your new car (I don't recommend it), be sure to check on the availability of promotional interest rates that may save you more money than the rebate. In those cases where you are offered a choice between the promotional interest rate and the rebate, you should sharpen up your pencil and do the arithmetic before you make your decision. The lower interest rate is sometimes the better deal.

Should I buy lottery tickets every week?

We all know people who buy $10, $20, or more in lottery tickets every week. (They may not let you in on their secret, but believe me, you do know such people.) Sadly, these people are usually the ones least able to afford such tomfoolery.

Gambling large sums of money makes it impossible to "always pay yourself first," the most important principle of sound money management. Spending inappropriate amounts of your money on lottery tickets or any other form of gambling is a self-destructive practice that makes no sense at all when examined in the cold light of day. This is the kind of behavior that can easily turn into a financially fatal addiction. Don't get started down that road. Once you do, you may find it difficult if, not impossible, to make a U-turn.

One financial management book I read devoted several pages of advice on what to do with your winnings if you hit it big in the lottery. You won't find that kind of advice here. You stand a much better chance of being killed by lightning than hitting the jackpot in the state lottery. It's that kind of blue-sky rambling that gets the unwary hooked on lottery fever.

While you're pondering that, start putting that $10 or $20 per week into investments that will make more dollars for you. If you've been taken in by that old chestnut, "you can't win if you don't play," fine. Spend $1 a week on a lottery ticket by giving up one coffee break a week. That way, you'll be "playing," at no cost and your odds of winning will be almost as good. More important, you'll be getting richer every day.

If that lone weekly ticket does turn out to be a winner of the big jackpot, give me a call. I'll tell you where I found all that advice about what to do with your millions.

Should I pay my income tax on my credit card?

In case you haven't heard, kindly old Uncle Sam wants to make it easier for you to pay your taxes. He will now accept payment on credit cards from three of the major issuers: Discover, MasterCard and American Express (At this writing, Visa is not yet a participant). Some taxpayers rejoiced at this news. Now they can earn frequent flier miles and other awards just by charging those big bucks that they have to pay anyway to their credit cards. Looks almost like found money.

And the response has tickled old Sam. By the first quarter of the year 2000, the number of taxpayers charging their taxes on credit cards was triple that of a year earlier, the first year of the program. And the number has been rising steadily ever since. According to American Express, the dollar amount of taxes charged to its card for the first quarter of 2000 was a whopping 900% over a year earlier. The average payment was $1,362. The largest single payment: $7.2 million.

But wait. Before you join the ecstatic throngs, there is something you ought to know: You will be charged a processing fee for the privilege.

No, the government doesn't charge the fee. It's assessed by Official Payments Corp., the company that handles the processing of tax payments by credit cards. According to the company, their fees are averaging about 2.5%. However, some taxpayers are paying substantially more or slightly less, depending on the size of their tax bill. (Wouldn't you love to know how much that guy with the $7.2 million tax bill was charged?)

For example, if you owe $1,000 in taxes and put it on your credit card, you'll pay a fee of $35. That's a whopping 3.5%, enough to make it likely that any awards you get from your credit card company will be more than offset by the fee. Pay a tax bill of $100 on your card and you'll be charged a fee of $6. That's 6%…a guarantee that you'll be in the hole.

If you're in the big bucks category and you owe $27,999 in taxes, you'd pay a processing fee of $699 for the privilege of charging it on your credit card. That's just a tad under 2.5%.

***

How you will make out in the processing fee-versus-awards derby depends on which credit card you use. The GM card is generally considered to have the most generous of the payback programs. It credits up to 5% of the charged amount to the future purchase of a General Motors car. But keep in mind that the most credit you can earn in one year is $500. That means that any amount charged to the card over $10,000 will earn no credit all. Remember that guy with the $7.2 million tax bill? I'll bet he didn't know that.

And don't forget the unyielding philosophy of those credit card issuers. On a $10,000 tax payment, the processing fee will be about $262. The $500 credit does give you a $238 advantage, but if you don't pay off the full balance right away, that profit will be quickly eaten up by the credit card finance charges you'll be paying every month.

Most or all of the other credit card issuers have less generous award programs, so they make it even tougher to make up for the processing fee. Even the airline cards that issue one frequent-flier mile for each dollar charged may not offer enough to offset the processing fee. Each frequent-flier mile has a cash value of about two cents. In most cases, that leaves you in the hole after paying the processing fee.

Some airlines offer double or triple miles for heavy travelers and that **might** make it possible to come out ahead. On the whole, though, paying Uncle Sam via credit card just isn't the great deal that it might appear to be at first blush.

And that brings us to the next principle of sound money management:

- **When it's time to pay your taxes, hide your credit card.**

If you're still not convinced, you can get more information at the Official Payments Corp. Web site, www.officialpayments.com. You can also see what Uncle Sam has to say about the subject at: www.irs.gov.

Should I "consolidate" my debts?

You've seen their ads on television. They are the debt consolidators who promise you economic salvation if only you will consolidate all of your debts with them.

Forget it. If you're already hopelessly bogged down in the debt quagmire, seek out a loan from any other legitimate source to consolidate your debts into a single payment. If you can borrow money at a lower interest rate than you are now paying, fine. Do it and pay off those old debts. At least you'll lower your interest costs.

But avoid the enticement of lower monthly payments spread out over a longer period. The only thing that ploy will do for you is sink you deeper into a never-ending morass of debt.

Should I sign up for one of those debit cards I've been hearing about?

Sure, if you lack self-discipline, and you don't mind giving up one of the best tools available to the smart money manager: taking advantage of the float.

To be sure, debit cards relieve you of the terrible chore of sitting down once a month to write a check to your credit card company. With a debit card, you never have to write a check because whatever you charge to the debit card is immediately and automatically charged (debited) to your bank account.

Debit cards look like credit cards, but they act just like checks. When you charge something to your debit card, an electronic genie immediately grabs the money out of your bank account and places it in the account of the card issuer.

Golly, what a great convenience. Of course, being relieved of writing a check once a month is going to cost you real money. So, our next principle of sound money management is:

- **The next time you receive a solicitation for a debit card, pass it through that new office shredder you just bought. If you already have a debit card, cut it up and replace it with an "old-fashioned" credit card.**

Sure, debit cards look, feel, and smell just like ordinary credit cards. They have the same degree of acceptance as credit cards. Furthermore, consumers are crazy about them. Ram Research, a Maryland-based credit research firm, estimates that Americans will make nearly 500 million purchases with them in 2000.

But, as P.T. Barnum pointed out, "Nobody ever went broke underestimating the intelligence of the American public." Come to think of it, wasn't he also the one who observed, "There's a sucker born every minute."

I'm not suggesting that you're a sucker if you use a debit card, only that you have better choices. Loss of the float isn't the only disadvantage. Don't forget the additional exposure to risk that comes with the debit card. It may look like an ordinary credit card, but if it's lost or stolen, the thief or finder can wipe out your entire bank account before you even know that it's gone.

Yes, once you report the theft and convince the bank that you aren't playing games, it will reimburse you for your losses. By then, though, your headaches will make you wish you'd never heard of debit cards.

Should I increase my payroll witholding so that I don't owe the IRS money every year at tax time?

If you ask Uncle Sam that question, you're likely to get an affirmative answer. After all, wouldn't it be nice not to have to write out a big check every year when income tax time rolls around? Wouldn't it be even better to get a healthy refund check instead?

Not if you're a savvy money manager.

Here's the real skinny on that deal. Every time you get a refund check from the IRS, you're simply getting your own money returned after giving the government an interest-free loan. That same money left in an interest-bearing account until tax time would be producing income that is yours to keep.

You wouldn't give that deadbeat brother-in-law an interest-free loan every year, would you? Well, why would you want to grant the same favor to a tax man whom you've never even met? When you hear someone bragging about his big income tax refund, you have my permission to call him an uniformed and undisciplined ninny (provided he doesn't outweigh you by 50 pounds).

How soon should I buy my first house?

Tomorrow, if possible.

Back in Chapter 5, we discussed the question of whether a home should be regarded as a financial investment. That's the kind of never-ending debate that's best left to the financial academicians. It's the sort of perennial argument they love, simply because it can never be proven in the same manner that two-plus-two can be proven. But make no mistake. If home ownership is in your long-range plans, you should make the decision to buy at the earliest time possible.

It's true that home ownership doesn't always represent the best possible investment from a strictly financial point of view (though it often does). However, there are other considerations that must be put into the mix.

Paying down that 20-year mortgage with those obligatory checks every month is a form of forced savings. For the fiscally undisciplined, of which there are millions among us, it often proves to be the only savings of any significance over a lifetime. For many people, perhaps most, the equity in their home is by far the largest portion of their net worth.

As I mentioned earlier, there are also psychological advantages in being a homeowner. For one thing, the stability and confidence that comes with owning your own home are strong enough to be a positive influence on other aspects of your life. Also, home ownership helps to establish you as a person of substance, both in the eyes of others and of yourself.

When you add it all up, the benefits of home ownership obliterate the theoretical arguments about whether or not it is a good investment.

If you need further persuasion of the importance of buying your home as early as possible, consider the comments in reply to the next decision. Remember, paying down that mortgage is a form of investment.

I've accumulated a couple of thousand dollars in savings. Should I start my investment program now or should I wait until I have more to invest?

The best answer I've ever seen to that question comes from financial guru Louis Rukeyser of TV's "Wall Street Week." He tells the story of two fictional investors, Ralph and his brother-in-law Darth.

The story begins with Ralph, the unluckiest investor in the entire world. Starting in 1963, Ralph invested $2,000 once a year into the stocks that comprise the Standard & Poor's 500 index. Ralph's timing was so astonishingly poor that he chose the worst day **every time**. Incredibly, he made his investment at the exact top of the market every year—and he kept that up for 10 years. After ten years, he just let his investment ride.

Despite his incredibly bad timing, as of March 1, 2000, Ralph's total investment of $20,000 had grown to a whopping $905,956.

Darth, the **luckiest** investor in the entire world invested his $2,000 at the absolute bottom of the market every year, an investor's wildest dreams come true. However, Darth didn't start his investing program until 1973, the year that Ralph quit. Darth was so lucky that he decided to keep up his investing for 20 years, investing twice as much for twice as long as Ralph.

But here's the kicker: As of that same March 1, 2000, Darth's investment of $40,000 was worth $28,014 less than Ralph's investment of $20,000—$877,942 vs. $905,956.

That's right. Lucky Darth invested twice as much money as Ralph for twice as long, yet Ralph was the clear winner.

If you don't get the moral of this story, let me put it in plain English. Start your investment program now! Not tomorrow. Not next week. Now. And forget market timing. Trying to outguess the market on timing is wasted energy. You can make more money just by getting started now and sticking to a faithful investing pattern.

A few minor decisions
Should I mail in the warranty card that came with my new appliance?

You've read the card over carefully. It says something like, "mail in this card to ensure proper warranty coverage for your new appliance,"

Sounds like you'd better take the time to fill it out and mail it in, lest you be denied warranty coverage.

Not so. Federal law prohibits companies from requiring the consumer to mail in a registration card in order to be protected under the warranty. The purpose of that card, pure and simple, is…marketing.

Did you notice all of the personal questions they asked you? Questions that seem to have nothing to do with the appliance? The information you provide on that card will give the company a marketing profile that they can use for their own marketing efforts or sell to other companies for the same purpose. If you don't mind being added to another bunch of junk mail lists, go ahead and fill it out. Otherwise, toss it. Your warranty coverage will not be affected in any way. Just be sure to save your receipt or other proof of purchase.

Should I agree to sign up for credit life insurance when I take out a loan?

In most cases, you should not. Credit life insurance is expensive, far more expensive than many other types of insurance. And there's more.

Credit insurance is offered to borrowers purportedly to protect them if they are unable to pay off their loans. Although it does offer some protection to you, the borrower, the prime beneficiary of such insurance is always the lender. If you die before you pay off your loan, the proceeds of the policy will go directly to the lender. Nothing goes to your estate, even though you paid the premiums.

Credit insurance is usually offered in a bundle which includes three different parts, credit life insurance, credit disability insurance, and credit involuntary unemployment insurance. In the event the borrower dies, or is disabled, or is involuntarily unemployed, the insurance company guarantees to either pay off the loan or make payments on the loan.

In actual practice, credit insurance companies deal directly with the lender, rather than the borrower who is paying for the insurance. Lenders agree to offer a chosen company's policies to the borrower. In return, the insurance companies offer a substantial commission to the lender on every policy written. The end effect of all this is that there is no practical way for the borrower to comparison shop for credit life insurance.

To muddy the waters further, the borrower is typically asked to accept or decline credit insurance coverage at the time he is being asked to sign a flurry of confusing documents. Usually, there will be no opportunity to choose among companies, or even among different policy options from the same company. The terms are often unclear, and many borrowers sign up for insurance without understanding that they have done so. The cost of the policy is obscured because the premium is financed as part of the loan itself. The total cost for all this can add up to hundreds of dollars even on a modest loan.

To add insult to injury, most companies won't insure borrowers over 65 or 70, the people most likely to use it.

In short, when you are taking out a loan, there often are only two choices about credit life insurance: Take it or leave it.

I say leave it.

Should I take out the insurance offered to me every time I rent a car?
There you are standing at the rental counter after waiting 20 minutes for your turn. After you've filled out all the paperwork, the agent asks if you want to accept or decline a list of various insurance coverages.

Just what you need at this point…another decision to make.

Deciding to accept or decline insurance on your rental car can be one of the most frustrating experiences on your trip. To make it tougher, the company will probably offer you four different types of coverage:

- Collision and Damage Waiver, which waives your deductible for the cost of repair to the vehicle in case of an accident.
- Personal Accident Insurance, insuring you against accidental death and medical expenses.
- Personal Effects Coverage, which covers your luggage and personal effects.
- Liability Insurance Supplement, insuring you if you are held liable for injury to others.

Then you find out that the company won't let you turn down the insurance just by saying no; they insist that you put your initials all over the form. That, of course, makes you worry that you may be making a serious mistake…in writing, no less.

That's all part of the game, of course. The psychological pressure to get you to sign is carefully orchestrated. As with everything else that people try to sell you, there is profit to be made if you say yes.

To make it even more complicated, provisions and coverage on policies can vary considerably from state to state, even with the same rental car company.

There is no easy answer here. I'm not going to say that you should or should not sign up. Every situation is different. One thing I can tell you is that the rental counter is no place for you to make this decision. You should do your homework before you leave on your trip.

You need to consider what type of insurance you already have, where you are driving, and what your "comfort level" will be if you decline coverage.

Start by reviewing your current auto insurance policy to determine what protection it gives you if you have an accident with a rental car.

About half the major insurance companies provide such coverage. That, of course, means that half don't.

Next, check to see if any of your credit cards provide additional coverage when you use them to pay for a rental. American Express, for example, provides automatic coverage for card holders who charge their car rentals to the American Express card.

If you're traveling on business, check to see if your employer carries insurance that covers you.

It's been my experience that most people have coverage under one or more of the categories above. I know I do, so I never pay the extra cost of insurance when I rent a car. If you already have coverage, it makes no sense to duplicate it.

In any event, I repeat that the rental counter is no place for you to be mulling over all of this. You should know what your decision will be before you leave on your trip. That way, if you decide to decline, you can go ahead and scrawl your initials all over that form without losing any sleep over it.

CHAPTER ELEVEN

Scams and Other Untidy Behavior

When a man with money meets a man with experience,
the man with experience will get the money,
and the man with the money will get some experience
—Anonymous

It is said that the two most powerful motivators in the human equation are fear and greed. No one understands this better than those shady characters who devote their lives to the job of separating other people from their money.

I know that sounds cynical. Nevertheless, you should never allow yourself to forget that there are people out there whose primary objective is, and always will be, to take whatever they can from you—legally or otherwise. And many of the scam artists scattered liberally throughout our population are remarkably successful at their craft. If they understand anything, it is the extraordinary power that can be wielded through skillful exploitation of the twin foibles of fear and greed.

What is most surprising, perhaps, is the perennial emergence of age-old, unlikely scams. Ancient deceits that you may think are so corny that no person of sound mind would fall for their outlandish premises.

On the opposite end of the spectrum are the new high-tech scams that depend on subtleties and the intricacies of modern technology to befuddle otherwise sensible people.

The pigeon drop

One ageless classic, the so-called "pigeon drop" scam has been around for generations. It's so old, its whiskers have whiskers.

When described in simple terms, the pigeon drop would appear to be so transparent that no rational person would be likely to fall for it. But don't kid yourself. This hoary old scam is successfully carried out all over the world in one form or another, year after year. And this year will be no exception.

The pigeon drop is usually pulled off by two women working as a team. One of the women approaches a likely-looking prospect on the street (most often an elderly woman just emerging from a bank). She strikes up a friendly conversation with the unsuspecting victim (pigeon). Soon the accomplice approaches the pair pretending to be a complete stranger. Feigning excitement, the scam artist produces a bag containing what appears to be a huge bundle of cash. "I just found this money on the street," she says to the pair, breathlessly. "There are tens of thousands of dollars here and I'm so excited I don't know what to do with it."

The con artist's partner peeks into the bag and pretends to see evidence that the money was gained through some illegal activity such as drugs or gambling. "I work for a lawyer," she says. "I'll call him and ask him what we should do."

In a few minutes she returns. "My lawyer says that we may keep the money and split it between us since it is illegal money," she says excitedly. "But we should each put up $3,000 to show that we can take care of our living expenses while we wait to see if anyone claims it."

Caught up in the excitement, the pigeon, who is near her bank, agrees to withdraw her share right away. When she comes out with the money and gives it to one of the partners, they agree to let her hold the bag full of money while they withdraw their share. When the women fail to return, the pigeon looks in the bag and sees that it has been switched and holds only wads of paper. Her own money, of course, is never seen again.

Despite the publicity afforded this scam over the years, it still works, proving only how some people will allow the notion of something-for-nothing to prevail over common sense.

People of all ages fall victim to scam artists, but the elderly are among their prime targets. If you or members of your family are enjoying the golden years, it's important to stay tuned-in to the dirty tricks that may come your way.

Like the pigeon drop, some scams committed against the elderly are like dandelions; they pop up every year in seeming contempt at efforts to wipe them out. According to one police official, scam artists go after the elderly because they have money and because they often make poor witnesses due to eyesight and memory problems.

Phony utility workers

Consider the case of Elizabeth, an 84-year-old woman who lives alone in Philadelphia. A man flashing what looked like a badge came to her door one day and said he was there to read her water meter. Obligingly, she let him in.

After she showed him where the meter was, he asked her to take him outside and show her how big her property was. They walked to the back fence where he engaged her in distracting conversation while his accomplices entered the house and ransacked its contents.

This incident took place in a city where local utilities and police have regularly publicized the fact that all utility workers carry photo ID, which they will show homeowners any time they knock on the door.

Officer Louis Sgro, a member of a special unit of the Philadelphia police department formed to combat crimes against the elderly says that the people who conduct this particular scam are often families of gypsies who travel from city to city. In one case, police seized $1.8 million plus several hundred thousand dollars in jewelry and collectibles from such a family. They had hidden their loot in safe deposit boxes in three states. Says Sgro of the elderly, "They're the most picked-on members of our society, bar none."

The thieves know that people who grew up during the depression often stash large amounts of money at home because of their mistrust of banks. People who are guilty of this foolish practice often feel that they have hidden their money in a clever spot where burglars can't find it.

But guess what? Professional burglars know all the clever hiding spots. They usually go right to where the money and valuables are with surprising efficiency.

Credit card scams

At the other end of the time scale are the new scams such as the one that depends on the trickster's ability to get the victim to divulge her credit card number. Often carried out on the telephone, the scam artist pretends to be a representative of a major credit card company or even a police detective. "We have evidence that someone is using your credit card without your knowledge," says the scam artist. "We may need your help to catch him before he ruins your credit."

This, understandably, will upset some people enough to cause a lapse of rational thinking. That's just the reaction the thief is looking for.

"We need to make certain that I'm talking to the right person," he says smoothly. "So please get out your credit card and read the number to me so that we can go right to work on this." Obligingly, the victim does as requested and the thief immediately starts to order merchandise using the victim's credit card number.

When this happens, the theft may not be uncovered until the victim gets her next statement and sees the fraudulent purchases. By that time, the thief has moved on to his next victim.

***

Many of today's credit card scams are directed **against** credit card companies, so we're not likely to be on the alert for scams conducted **by** credit card companies. But, according to some credit card users, it does happen.

Perhaps scam is too harsh a word for it, but there is one practice that certainly comes under the heading of untidy behavior. It involves what many people believe to be the deliberate mailing of credit card bills to arrive just a few days before the due date. The idea being that you probably won't have time to mail your payment in quickly enough to avoid a late-payment fee.

Issuers of credit cards are required by law to mail bills at least two weeks before the due date and to process incoming payments immediately upon receipt. However, some consumer advocates say that a few companies may be sending out their bills to arrive at the last possible moment. Then they process the payments so slowly that late-fees are generated. This, critics say, increases the company's revenues and profits at the consumers' expense.

The credit card companies, of course, deny such allegations. They blame slow mail delivery and people who allow their mail to sit around for days before they open it.

This whole business falls "somewhere between a scam, a scandal and a rip-off," says Robert Heady, founder of the Bank Rate Monitor research firm.

The truth about all this may never be known for certain. That's because most credit card issuers use bulk mail imprinted with bar codes to send out their bills. That category of mail carries no dated postmark, making it impossible for the consumer to determine when the bill was mailed.

In any event, late payments can cost you in two big ways. First is the hefty late payment fee. Then there is the negative credit report that can classify you as a higher credit risk. That, in turn, will increase the interest rate charged on your credit card purchases.

And that brings us to the next principle of sound money management:

- **Examine your incoming credit cards carefully to determine the due date. Make certain that you mail in your payments in time to beat the deadline.**

What happens if you fall victim to a late-billing scam (or you just get careless) and get nailed with a late-payment fee? The good news is that most companies will remove the charge if you complain promptly, provided you have a good payment history. I found a $29 late-payment fee on my account a couple of years ago; it was removed without hesitation when I called to complain. Consumer groups report similar experiences.

But that's not all that you must remain on the lookout for in your relationship with your credit card companies.

Imagine this: You have a hefty balance on your credit card, several thousand dollars or more and you've been paying a whopping 19.5% interest. You've seen the light, however, and that 19.5% is grating on your insides. Now you're actively trying to pay off the balance to get out from under that load.

Then one day you receive a pleasant letter from the credit card company. "We've noticed that you're trying to pay off your balance and we want to help you," says the letter. "We're going to lower your interest rate to 15.9%. There is no catch. All you have to do is call us and tell us to go ahead. After all, it's good business for us to help you pay down your credit card debt."

What a nice gesture. This must be a company with a heart.

Don't you believe it.

Credit card companies make their big bucks from people who carry large balances and pay the minimum each month at the highest rate the company can charge. Every customer who falls into that mold is solid gold to them. So why would they want to help you to pay off your debt with a voluntary reduction in the interest rate you are already paying?

They don't. The cynical idea behind all this is that they hope their kind gesture will cause you to lose your motivation to pay off the balance. After all, a monthly interest fee of 15.9% is a lot better than no interest fee at all, which is what they get if you pay off the balance.

As transparent as all this seems, it must work. Lots of people fall for it, and some probably brag about their financial savvy in doing so.

Some financial advisors see this situation as an indication that interest fees from credit card companies may be more flexible than we know. They suggest calling your company and asking for a reduction in their interest charge if they want to keep your business. What can you lose? It just might work.

Best of all, though, you should do everything in your power to pay off that balance in full. Once it's wiped off the books, keep it off by paying the full balance every month. Eliminating an interest charge of 19.5% or 15.9% is the same thing as getting a return of 19.5% or 15.9% on your money. Better you get it than the credit card company.

Internet scams

When it comes to scams, there is arguably no more fertile ground than the marvelous new world of the Internet. Cyberspace holds unlimited stores of information on anything about anything. Entertainment, financial advice, convenient shopping, romance, grief counseling, humor, just about any subject that you can dream up can be found on the Web.

Most of the nooks and crannies you discover on the web will be legitimate, though dull and boring. You'll find teenagers' home pages and photos of granddad's children. You'll also find a huge number of online shopping sites, places where you can order just about anything you could want, all from the convenience of your own home.

Unfortunately, the Internet also plays host to what is arguably the greatest collection of scam artists ever to operate under the same umbrella. The Internet allows any company or individual to communicate instantly with millions of people with very little effort or money—a scam artist's dream come true. It's easy to craft Internet pages that look credible and legitimate. They can make it next to impossible for investors or customers to be certain of what is fact and what is fiction.

As an investor, you will want to be especially careful of Web sites that offer "hot" investing tips. Always keep in mind that the Internet is freedom of speech to the ultimate. Anyone can put just about anything on a Web site. One of the most popular scams on the Internet involves the placing of false information about a company in order to drive up the price of its stock momentarily. When the suckers rush to buy it, driving up the price of the stock, the perpetrators sell their holdings and move on.

That's why you must never make an investment based solely on what you've seen or read on the Internet, and that includes online newsletters or bulletin board postings.

The likelihood of investor fraud in the Internet increases as you go from the large, closely regulated markets such as the New York Stock Exchange and NASDAQ to the smaller, less-regulated markets. Before you invest in so-called penny stocks (now generally taken to mean stocks that sell for less than $5 per share) you should check in at the Securities and Exchange Commission's Edgar database at www.sec.gov. There you'll be able to examine the company's public filings. Before tying up with a new broker, you may want to check on the disciplinary record of both the broker and the broker's company at www.nasdr.com.

Which brings us to the next principle of sound money management:

- Never forget that "hot" tips on the Internet are just as worthless as those hot tips you get from friends and neighbors.

Fortunately most shopping sites on the Web are quite legitimate, but there is also a healthy share of out and out scams to watch out for. Be alert in particular for price and service offers that are unrealistic. Remember the old adage, if it sounds too good to be true, it almost certainly is. In particular, avoid amateurish sites that offer impossibly low prices and no direct telephone access.

Even when you are shopping at the finest, most reputable sites, you should think about what will happen if the merchandise arrives broken or not working properly. How is merchandise exchanged? Who will pay for the shipping? Exactly what kind of guarantee will you get?

Shopping the old-fashioned way at your local store may seem dull by comparison, but when trouble brews you know that all you have to do is schlepp back to the customer service desk at the store. It's not that simple in cyberspace.

Fortunately, you needn't worry about having your credit card numbers stolen when you shop on the Web, provided the site you buy from is using a "secure" server. Secure server technology scrambles all information you enter into a garbled mess that makes it undecipherable by anyone except the intended receiver. This system is all but fool proof and virtually all serious e-commerce sites use it.

A more serious concern, at least for some people, is the privacy issue. Internet technology allows vendors to gather huge amounts of personal information about users. Although most legitimate retailers have at least some form of privacy policy, their value is arguable. If you're not concerned about data being compiled on such things as your personal statistics and shopping habits, that's fine. But be aware that this practice is widespread and growing.

Using the Internet for shopping is certain to become more popular as these problems are minimized in the future. In the meantime, be careful, the dollar you save may be your own.

***

How about that great Internet service that we have come to call e-mail. Could that be another vehicle used by scam artists to separate you from your money? The answer is a resounding "yes." In fact, if you have an e-mailbox, you almost certainly have been the recipient of e-mail missives with evil intent.

The Federal Trade Commission recently identified the 12 scams most likely to wind up in your e-mailbox. Let's call them the "Dirty Dozen."

1. **Business opportunities.** If you don't already know that any unsolicited mail offering to show you how to make thousands of dollars with little or no effort is a sham, shame on you. The only people who make money on these pyramid schemes are the people who invent them.

2. **Bulk e-mail lists.** It's easy to buy lists of e-mail addresses by the millions. Some ads would have you believe that sending out your own solicitations to the lists they will sell you is a sure road to wealth. Forget it. Sending unsolicited e-mail violates the terms of most Internet service providers. The practice may result in you being cut off by your ISP. Worse, you could find yourself in legal hot water for violating new laws springing up in a number of states.

3. **Chain letters.** Can you believe that there are still people around who fall for this ancient scam? The letter asks you to send a small amount of money to the first four or five names on the list, replace one of the names with your own and forward the letter via bulk e-mail.

These letters are almost always illegal, even the ones that claim they are legal. More important, nearly everyone who participates will lose money to the originator of the letter.

4. **Work-at-home schemes.** It's a shame. Shut-ins, elderly people, busy housewives; these are the people most often targeted by ads promising high earnings for such menial jobs as addressing envelopes or simple craft assemblies. Often these schemes require you to invest hundreds of dollars to buy equipment needed to turn out the products that the company promises to buy. The most frequent result: The company refuses to buy your products claiming that your work isn't up to their high standards.

5. **Health and diet scams.** Stop and think about it. If someone invented or discovered a solution to one of society's most distressing problems, the world would be clamoring at their door. Lose weight without exercising, grow a new head of hair, cure cancer or arthritis. Find a way to do these things and you won't have time to send out petty ads on bulk e-mail.

6. **Effortless income.** C'mon. You know hard it is to make a buck. If it were easy to make money without working, everybody would be doing it. Take that newsletter describing lots of easy ways to make money and toss it in the trash. If the wise guy who publishes that stuff knew a legal way to make $4,000 in a single day, he sure wouldn't be telling you about it.

7. **Free goods.** Get it in your head. No one is going to offer the public valuable goods for free. When you get an e-mail message offering such valuable stuff as a free computer, TV or long distance phone card for the asking, delete it at once. Most of these scams are just pyramid schemes that allow you to earn the free goods (instead of money) by bringing in other suckers. The only people who profit from this scam are the promoters.

8. **Investment opportunities.** Understand one thing: In the investment world, return is tied directly and immutably to the degree of risk

involved. The greater the risk, the higher the return; the lower the risk, the lower the return. When you see an investment opportunity offering an outrageously high rate of return with no risk, you're about to be had. Whether the offer involves forming an offshore bank, buying real estate at giveaway prices or an opportunity to benefit from "inside information," run, don't walk, to the nearest exit.

9. **Cable descrambler kits.** Modestly priced kits that are supposed to allow you to receive cable transmissions without paying a monthly fee probably won't work. Even if they do, you'll be violating the law if you use one. Stealing service from a cable TV company can land you in jail.

10. **Guaranteed loans or credit on easy terms.** Offers to get you home equity or other types of loans even if you have terrible credit are often a booby trap for unsuspecting individuals. After you pay a fee for the service, you'll probably just get a list of lenders who will turn you down. Don't try to find the perpetrators, they'll probably be gone by the time you find out you've been had.

11. **Credit repair.** In my view, this is one of the most cynical of the consumer frauds, since it preys on people who are already in over their heads. Promises to erase your bad credit history can't be fulfilled. It's going to take time and hard work to clear your history if you've developed a bad credit record.

No company can erase that history with or without a fee. Further, some of these outfits may subject you to serious legal problems by suggesting that you lie on a loan application or misrepresent your Social Security number.

12. **Vacation prize promotions.** You've been specially selected to receive a free or very low-cost vacation. Yeah, right. And so have the millions of other people who received this e-mail scam. If you bite, the cruise ship you're booked on may be a broken down tugboat. The hotel you'll stay at may be a filthy flea-bag. And you'll find that additional "fees" may well cost you more than a legitimate package vacation.

If you feel you've been victimized by any of the consumer frauds listed here, or by any new ones that they haven't heard about, you should file a complaint with the FTC. Contact the Consumer Response Center by phone at 1-877-382-4357; by mail at Consumer Response Center, Federal Trade Commission, 600 Pennsylvania Ave. NW, Washington, D.C. 20580; or through the Internet at http://www.ftc.gov.

The FTC cannot resolve your individual problem, but it can take action against a company if it learns of a pattern of possible law violations.

The FTC web site is just one of thousands, perhaps millions, that can help you to deal with almost any subject imaginable. In fact, the Internet holds just about all the information in the world—good and bad, true and false, important and trivial. But remember it's up to you to know the difference.

One way to learn that difference is to log on to a great web site dedicated to wiping out Internet scams: http://www.scambusters.org/. Check in with Scambusters on a regular basis and you'll soon know more about Internet scams than you ever wanted to know.

Mail scams

Could our beloved United States Postal Service be guilty of helping some scam artists to separate you from your money? You bet, but don't blame the USPS. They're doing their best to nail thieves who use the mails to cheat you.

Typical of the scams that can reach you in your regular mail box is the infamous Nigerian letter. The writer of the letter, mailed from Nigeria, claims to have acquired or legally seized millions of dollars or several trunks of silver or gold worth millions. The writer says he desperately wants to move the money to a safe country and is willing to pay one-third of it (several million dollars) to anyone who will help him. If you will simply respond to the letter, this illicit windfall will be yours.

If you answer the letter, you will soon receive another explaining that the writer needs expense money to get the loot out of Nigeria and into your hands. You may keep one third of the money and the writer will show up to claim the other two-thirds. Of course, if you send the expense money, you'll never see it again, nor will you ever receive a package from Nigeria.

Frankly, if you fall for this one, or any of the many variations of it, I think you're a sheep who deserves to be shorn.

Home improvement scams

One of the most persistent and lucrative scams most often directed against the elderly is the driveway caper. In the typical version, a man knocks on the door and says he's a driveway contractor doing work in the neighborhood and couldn't help but notice that the victim's driveway is in serious need of resurfacing. Since their equipment is already in the area, they are in a position to offer a fabulous deal on resurfacing.

If the victim falls for it, the perpetrators quickly spread a thin tar coating over the driveway which makes it look shiny and new for a few days or until it rains, whichever comes first. This "repair" job, which took a few dollars worth of thin tar mix, will cost the victim hundreds or perhaps thousands of dollars. By the time the scam is obvious, the perpetrators will be far away and literally untraceable.

Of course, the driveway caper is only one of many versions of household scams. The next most popular one involves the roof. Same idea, same technique, but usually a lot more money.

How can you avoid these costly household scams? First of all, your red flags must unfurl quickly whenever some tradesman offers you a deal that is good "for today only." Never sign up for an improvement project without two or three estimates from reliable local concerns. That's standard practice. Any legitimate tradesman understands that and will offer no resistance to it. Any time a vendor attempts to discourage you from getting another estimate, show him the door.

Be especially wary of pickup trucks with those little magnetic signs that can be stuck on the side of any vehicle and quickly removed. Look for trucks that are clearly lettered with a company name and (local) phone number. Never sign a contract without reading it first.

Telephone scams

You should be aware that telephone company technicians do not need to call you to ask for help in checking your telephone line. All their work can be done from remote locations and they are **never** going to call you and ask that you dial a certain number and then hang up. This kind of telephone scam can make it possible for the caller to gain access to your phone line and then make unlimited long distance calls on your phone bill. This scam seems to originate mostly from penal institutions where inmates are happy to chat with friends on your nickel.

Other variations of this scam are carried out when the victim receives an urgent phone, pager, or e-mail message asking her to call a certain long distance number for "urgently important" news. This news supposedly involves family members who are ill, in jail, or otherwise in need of help. The victim isn't aware that the number she is asked to call is an overseas number. When the bill arrives, the charge for the call is as much as $100. The people who pull off this scam are apparently given a percentage of the charges billed by their local phone companies.

This scam originated in the Dominican Republic (area code 809) but his since spread throughout many Caribbean countries including but not limited to: The Bahamas (242), Bermuda (441), Barbados (246), Jamaica (876), Cayman Islands (345) and Trinidad (868).

This dirty trick is made possible by the fact that the international telephone communications treaty permits each country to establish its own telephone rates. Thus, the per-minute charge can be set at outrageous levels. Recently, similar scams have originated in several Eastern European countries. Almost any country with a three-digit area code could become a breeding ground for this dirty trick, so be advised.

Protect your Social Security Number

Hundreds of military officers became victims of credit card fraud just because their Social Security numbers were published in the *Congressional Record*. That's how sensitive your Social Security number is.

Never give out your number to anyone on the telephone under any circumstances. Further, don't give it out to anyone or any organization that doesn't need to have it. Legitimate organizations such as banks, insurance companies and government agencies may need it. Think twice before you give it to anyone else, and never put documents containing your number in the trash. Shred them, cut them up or burn them. There is no easier way to steal your identity than to obtain your Social Security number.

Speaking of scams conducted by telephone, there is no better illustration of preposterous gullibility than the story of a prison inmate we'll call Joe. Working entirely from inside a Pennsylvania prison, Joe used his access to a prison telephone to scam more than $100,000 from 58 victims across the country. How? He simply used an outside accomplice to obtain credit card numbers. Then, he called the credit card companies and talked their operators into giving him personal-access codes and expiration dates for the names involved. Using that tactic, he assembled all the information he needed to order 37 new credit cards with a total credit limit exceeding $900,000.

How in heaven's name could trained credit card company operators be conned into giving out that kind of information? Don't ask me. When I call trying to get information about my own account, they won't even talk to me until I tell them my entire family history and that of my next door neighbor as well. And how could a prisoner stay on the telephone for up to 10 hours a day without causing anyone in authority to wonder what he was up to? Go figure.

By now, you have the idea. This litany of scams and untidy behavior could go on endlessly. But it can all be summed up briefly. Wherever you are, whoever you are, there's someone out there who would like to relieve you of your money. There may not be any sure-fire vaccination against scam artists, but there are a couple of common sense guidelines that you would do well to keep in mind:

- First and most important, don't let greed get the best of you. Any time someone convinces you that you can get something for nothing, you're ripe for the picking.
- Next, don't trust strangers who attempt to engage you in any transaction involving money.
- Don't give out your Social Security number.
- Finally, never fall for the line that "this fantastic offer is good for today only."

CHAPTER TWELVE

Preparing for Retirement

You can be young without money but you can't be old without it.
—Tennessee Williams (1914–1983)

Is it too early for you to be thinking about retirement? Are you too young to be concerned about life after you've kissed your boss goodbye forever?

I hope you know the answers to those questions by now.

The younger you are when you start applying the basic principles of sound money management, the better your chances of accumulating the kind of money you'll need to enjoy the good life in your leisure years. A million dollars may seem like a lot of money to you now. However, if you're young, say under 40, even a million bucks won't be enough to live like royalty by the time you reach retirement age. If you're older than 40 and haven't yet stashed away that million dollars, you'd better get to work today.

Retirement will sneak up on you faster than you could ever imagine. When it does arrive, it can be one of the most carefree, fun-filled times of your life...or one of the most dreadful. Which way it turns out for you will depend almost entirely on how well you prepare for it.

A retirement free of financial worries is a blessing; a retirement spent in debilitating worry about how to keep up with the relentless increases in the cost of everything you need to survive can be a living hell. If you don't think so, just ask someone who is struggling to make it on Social Security and perhaps a small pension.

Whether your age is 25 or 55, the most important question you need to ask about your retirement is: How much income will I need to maintain my present lifestyle?

Unless you're a CPA who specializes in retirement planning, you probably don't have a clue. Unfortunately, most people don't think much about the subject until retirement time looms just over the horizon. By then, it's often too late to take the simple steps that can assure a comfortable and rewarding life of leisure.

Most financial planners say that you will need 80% of your pre-retirement income in order to maintain your current lifestyle in retirement. If you earn, say, $60,000 per year just prior to your retirement, you will need $48,000 to maintain the same lifestyle. If your annual income is $100,000, you'll need $80,000 per year to retire in the style to which you have become accustomed.

That kind of income isn't going to appear out of thin air. If you expect to enjoy a comfortable retirement, you're going to have to arrange for it yourself. That point cannot be over-stressed. No one else is going to worry about your financial health in retirement—not your employer, not your banker, not your brother-in-law, not your old English teacher. If you don't take care of it yourself, it won't happen.

And keep this in mind: When it comes to estimating your need for retirement income, you are far more likely to underestimate your need than overestimate it. If there are any financial surprises, they probably will be unpleasant ones.

***

Preparation for achieving your financial goals in retirement begins—or should begin—on the day you leave school and take your first full-time job. If you haven't noticed it, this theme has been subtly woven throughout the fabric of this book. Living life for all its worth when you are young is a perfectly acceptable philosophy. Still, it takes only a little extra effort to ensure that same comfort level after you leave the working world behind.

The bottom line: If you don't take care of this little matter yourself, no one else will do it for you.

Yes, yes, I know that you have Social Security. But all you can count on from that government program is a little gravy. Have you ever tried to eat a plate of gravy by itself? I don't think so. Please keep that ugly picture in mind as a reminder that you're going to have to provide the meat and potatoes of retirement yourself.

The good news is that the U.S. Congress has made it easier than ever to feather your retirement nest. They've laid out a menu of attractive retirement programs that earlier generations could hardly have dreamed of. Still, they're not going to do the work for you. You have to do it for yourself. If you've put the principles in this book to work, you've already made a good start. But there's more work to do. And that brings us to the next principle of sound money management:

- **You must participate to fullest possible extent in every government approved retirement program available to you.**

It simply isn't possible to overstate the importance of this principle. Never before in our country's history has it been easier to take control of your own retirement finances. Still, every one of these golden opportunities requires action from you to get the ball rolling.

Back in 1918, when officials at Sears, Roebuck and Co. announced their new pension plan, it was viewed as a radical new idea. Instead of the traditional formula where the company invested money on behalf of the workers and then paid the retirees a set amount in retirement, Sears set up a new plan. Their profit-sharing pension plan allowed both the company and the employee to contribute a fixed percentage of each employee's wages into the employee's individual retirement account.

This was the first defined contribution retirement program, and only one company offered it.

Today, every employee may choose from a variety of retirement programs authorized and monitored by the federal government. As with the Sears plan, though, nothing happens until the employee (you) takes action. Before you can enjoy the benefits of a good retirement program, you must take the first step by signing up for it.

The 401(k) Plan

Are you an employee with at least one year and a minimum of 1,000 hours of service? If you are, you're eligible for what is arguably the best retirement plan among the smorgasbord available to today's workers. It's called 401(k) and almost every large company and many smaller ones now offer some version of it to their employees.

If your company has a 401(k) plan and you haven't opted to join, shame on you. You're throwing money away. If you are participating, congratulations. You've made what may be one of your wisest financial decisions.

What more could you ask? Tax deductible contributions, all income tax-deferred until you retire, portability if you change employers, plus additional contributions from your employers. Imagine...your employer making regular deposits to YOUR account. What would Ebenezer Scrooge have to say about that?

As a participant in a 401(k), you may deposit a percentage of your earnings (determined by your employer's plan) each year. In addition, your employer may kick in with 15%, 50%, even 100% or more of the amount you contribute.

Make no mistake. This is found money. It adds even more reason for you to participate to the fullest permissible extent in your company's 401(k) program.

The combined total of your own and your employer's contribution may not exceed 15% of your earnings up to a specified dollar amount.

The maximum amount for the year 2000 was $10,500. This amount increases periodically to allow for inflation. The limit on contributions has been set to make sure that higher paid employees don't participate to a disproportionate degree over those with lower earnings.

You don't have to contribute the full permissible maximum. You may put in any lesser amount up to the maximum. Given the power of the 401(k), however, you should do whatever is possible to maximize your contribution. To do less is to let your employer and Uncle Sam off the hook.

Many younger employees decline the opportunity to participate in a 401(k) plan because they "can't afford it." If you feel that way, please remember that the relatively painless system of payroll deductions is used to collect your contributions. Since you never see the money, it somehow makes it easier to live without it. You'll make out just fine without it, and you'll be building a strong base for a financially secure future.

Tax-deferred retirement accounts allow you to harness the almost unimaginable power of compounding with a special kicker—the tax man is held at bay. But you have to take the initiative; you have to take action; you have to sign up. Until you do, you are the loser.

There's a great deal more to 401(k) plans than I can cover here, and legislative changes are always a consideration. For the most part, you'll have to rely on your employer for information regarding the specific flavor offered by your company. However, if you're an Internet prowler, you'll want to log on the Web site that contains more information about 401(k) plans that you ever wanted to know: www.401(k)afe.com. Talk about straight from the horse's mouth, this site lets you pose questions to the man who invented the 401(k).

If you're digitally challenged but still want to know more about 401(k) plans, get yourself a copy of *The Complete Idiot's Guide to 401(k) Plans* by Bogosian & Lee (Alpha Books). I like this one because it gets to the point without a lot of verbiage.

However you approach it, the bottom line is this: If you're qualified to join a 401(k) plan and haven't yet taken the step, do it now. Every day that you delay is costing you money.

Employee Stock Ownership Plans (ESOPs)

If you are an employee, you may find yourself being offered an ESOP instead of a 401(k). If your employer happens to be the next Microsoft, you've struck it rich. Sign up immediately and throw this book away; you won't be needing it.

Of all the defined contribution retirement plans, the ESOP appears on the surface to be the most glamorous. The company deposits shares of its stock into your retirement account in your name. If the price of the stock skyrockets, you could become very rich. Many people have.

So what's the catch?

For openers, if the company goes broke, so will your retirement. Even if the company does well, you won't be able to make any withdrawals from your account until you retire or leave the company. Unless the company's stock is publicly held and listed on a stock exchange, you won't even know what it's worth without getting an appraisal from an expert. And your expert may not know any more about it than you do.

Problems like these explain why these accounts have not been met with a great deal of enthusiasm by the general population of employees. They're very popular with companies, though, because they provide a bundle of tax breaks for the employer.

If you're already enrolled in an ESOP and it's clear that your company's stock is risky at best, there are several things you can do to ease the pain. You might want to keep your eye peeled for a better job, dissolve your account, and roll the proceeds over into an IRA. (Be prepared, however. Some companies may drag out this process for as much as several years after you leave.)

If you plan to stay with the company, the law allows you a couple of options. When you reach age 55, you can demand that the company diversify your account by investing 25% of your stock into the stock of other companies, or some entirely different form of investment.

That figure increases to 50% by the time you reach age 60. This allows you to diversify an account that otherwise is probably 100% invested in the stock of your employer's company.

Depending on your earnings, you may also be entitled to open an IRA account even if you participate in an ESOP. If you qualify, open that IRA and participate to the fullest possible degree. This could prove to be your best insurance for a tidy nest egg at your retirement.

Traditional Individual Retirement Account (IRA)

The granddaddy of the federally-sponsored retirement programs is the traditional Individual Retirement Account (IRA). For many years, the IRA—contributions to which are also tax-deductible—was the only choice. Today, employees may opt for the traditional or the newer and better Roth IRA. Both offer excellent ways to build solid retirement income, but the differences are significant. You should consider them carefully if you are eligible and haven't yet opened an IRA.

You may open a traditional tax-deductible IRA if you are not a participant in a company retirement plan. For the most part that would mean your company has no retirement plan, since most company plans would offer you more benefits than you would get from either form of IRA.

Even if you do participate in a company retirement plan, you are eligible to open a tax-deductible IRA if your adjusted gross income is below a specified limit. As of this writing, the limit is $25,000 for single persons and $40,000 for marrieds. This limit will rise each year until 2005 when it tops out at $50,000 for singles and $65,000 for marrieds.

You may deposit up to $2,000 each year into your IRA and the full amount is deductible on your federal income tax. With your new understanding of the important difference between before-tax and after-tax dollars, you know how valuable this feature can be. Every year that you qualify, you may deposit an additional $2,000 in your account where your money will grow on a tax-deferred basis until you reach retirement age.

Your spouse may also open a tax-deductible IRA and deposit a maximum of $2,000 even if he or she is not employed. The numbers of Americans who qualify for this additional IRA but do not take advantage of it is clear evidence of how many people simply are unaware of what they are losing. I hope that you are not one of them.

IRAs that are started early in your career will grow to substantial sums while providing you with that delicious tax deduction that compounds the value of your contribution. Even older wage earners can add substantially to their ultimate wealth and enjoy the special benefits of tax deferred earnings by opening an IRA account.

Is it difficult to open an IRA account? Absolutely not. Just visit your local bank or a brokerage firm. They'll be happy to set up your account and explain the rules and your options.

The Roth IRA

The newest version of the Individual Retirement Program is called the Roth IRA. The Roth differs from the traditional in one very important way: Contributions to a Roth are NOT tax deductible as they are in the traditional IRA. But hold on. Here's the good part. Just as in the regular IRA, The money in your Roth IRA accumulates tax free. Even better, you may make withdrawals at any time without a penalty.

But the best feature of all, the feature that makes the Roth IRA a better choice than the traditional IRA, is that you won't owe a penny of taxes on your withdrawals. That's right. The money in your account compounds tax-free and you won't owe a penny of tax when it's time to start withdrawing.

The consequences of this arrangement are profoundly important to your future. This tax-free withdrawal privilege is regarded by many financial professionals as the most important financial tool in your retirement toolbox.

You may deposit up to $2,000 per year in your Roth IRA, and it is possible for you to have a Roth even if you also have a regular IRA. Check with your accountant to make sure you qualify. If you already have a traditional IRA, it is possible to convert it to a Roth. Everyone's situation is different, so you will want to discuss your situation with your accountant or other knowledgeable advisor.

As with other federally-sponsored retirement programs, Roth IRA rules are complex and subject to change. One of the best ways to keep up to date with the bureaucrats' tendencies to fix things that ain't broke is to log on to www.rothira.com. Here you'll find the latest news as well as access to scores of articles written by experts on the subject.

Retirement Plans for the Self-Employed

If you're self-employed, not to worry; there are variations of the above plans designed especially for you. They're arguably even more valuable than are those for employees. And don't forget, any type of self-employment income qualifies you to participate.

Let's say that you're a full-time employee and that you operate a little moonlighting business out of your home. Even if you are participating in a retirement plan through your employer, you may still open up your own self-employed account based on your moonlighting income. Do this early on and even your part-time retirement account will help to make your retirement years golden.

Keogh Plans

The original retirement plan for the self-employed (Keogh) has been outclassed in many ways by later variations. Still, it's a good bet for entrepreneurs with substantial income.

A so-called profit-sharing Keogh allows you to contribute a nominal 15% of your earning to the plan. Actually, because of some esoteric mathematical calculations dreamed up by those nameless bureaucrats, the actual figure is more like 12% to 13%. If you're into self-flagellation, here's the formula: Reduce 15% of your self-employment income by half of your self-employment (Social Security) tax, and then subtract the amount you'll contribute to the plan.

Yes, yes, I know. In order to figure out how much you MAY contribute, you have to know how much you WILL contribute. Blame Washington, not me. Fortunately, it works out the same if you simply reduce your earnings by half of your self-employment tax and multiply by 13.043%

To complicate matters further, there is a cap on the amount of earning you can use for the calculations. That amount will be adjusted each year for inflation.

If you're a sane and rational person who wants to stay that way while still enjoying the benefits of a Keogh plan, tear this page out of the book, throw it away, and call an accountant. They get paid to absorb this kind of cruel punishment.

Another variation of the Keogh is called the money-purchase plan. If your self-employment income is in the big buck range, this is your best choice. It allows you to put away more money than the profit-sharing Keogh, up to 25% of your earnings.

The catch? You must designate a percentage of your income that you will contribute to your account each year and stick with it. If you find yourself unable to make the designated contribution in a given year, you'll owe a penalty. The IRS may make an exception under certain hardship conditions, but this is still a major consideration that you must take into account if you're thinking about setting up a money-purchase plan.

The calculations for the money-purchase plan are similar to those for other Keoghs. That nominal 25% contribution allowed by the plan will figure out to more like 20% in the real world. Still, that's a substantial figure that could allow you to build a huge kitty at retirement time.

If you set up a Keogh plan and you have employees, it's important to understand that you are required to make contributions for your employees too. However, you do have some protection from the hassles and paperwork that might result from employees who come and go after short service. The regulations permit you to set up your plan so that only employees with three years of continuous service are eligible to join the plan.

Simplified Employee Pensions (SEPs)

Fortunately there is now a special version of the IRA that opens the door for your golden retirement without the burden of all the mind-numbing paperwork required by the Keogh plans. The Simplified Employee Pension (SEP) is clearly the first choice for most self-employed individuals. As an entrepreneur you may open a SEP account and deposit 15% (using the same calculations required by the Keogh) of your self-employment income up to a designated maximum per year. (This amount will also be increased from year-to-year to allow for inflation.)

The SEP requires no costly paperwork, allows you to contribute any amount each year up to the maximum. You may even skip a year, if you like, without any penalty. SEP plans are much easier for small companies to set up and administration is painless and low cost.

All of the self-employed retirement plans have similar rules regarding withdrawals. There is a 10% penalty for any withdrawals made before age 59½ and you must begin mandatory withdrawals at age 70½.

The IRS (800-829-3676) will send you free booklets on any of the above plans. For SEPs and Keoghs, ask for Publication 560. For IRAs, ask for Publication 590.

***

Retirement plans such as those described above are marvelous ways to help brighten your path to those golden years. Still, as you approach that time of life and begin to take stock of your financial foundation, be advised that you may not have amassed as much as you think, thanks to those ubiquitous income taxes.

While all that money has been building up in your tax-deferred retirement account, you may have forgotten something: It's tax-deferred, not tax free (except for the Roth IRA). The day of reckoning comes when you reach age 70½ and must begin mandatory withdrawals. That's when you realize that as much as one-third or more of your tax-deferred nest egg will eventually be going to Uncle Sam. Remember, tax-deferred is good, but it's not tax-free.

Suppose for a moment that you were fortunate enough to have $500,000 in a tax-deferred account. Let's suppose, too, that your good friend, Joe, also has managed to accumulate $500,000, but his is in a taxable account with taxes on capital gains paid as they were generated. Who is the richest? You guessed it. Joe has a lot more money than you have. So, as you lay out your plans for retirement, keep in mind that those tax deferred accounts, as wonderful as they are, will add less to your net worth than appears at first blush.

Want to do your retirement planning the lazy man's way? If you can find your way around a computer keyboard, the latest generation of retirement planning software may be just what the doctor ordered. Some of the better programs will help you to set retirement goals such as the amounts you need to save. Many also provide help in choosing the investment vehicles most likely to produce the results you're after.

In my view, the best programs are the ones that take a conservative approach when estimating the amounts you'll have to stash away and how much of a return you can realistically expect. You don't want to launch a retirement plan that depends on getting a 20% return every year for 20 years, or one that suggests that you can maintain your lifestyle with 60% of your current income. You can't do either.

The two most popular programs for handling overall personal finances (Quicken, $60 and Microsoft Money, $70) also include retirement planning features that are quite helpful. I prefer *Quicken*, but that may be simply because I am more familiar with it than I am with *Money*.

Dedicated retirement programs—software that has only one purpose—may be a better bet for you, even if you use one of the personal finance programs for general financial management. Among the programs rated very high by software reviewers are:

- Kiplinger's Net Wealth (Block Financial) $30
- Financial Tools (Vorton Technologies) $20
- Plan Retirement Quick and Easy (Individual Software) $20
- Retire Secure (PricewaterhouseCoopers) $15

How good are these programs? How accurate and helpful will they be? To a large measure, that depends on you. You've got to be both accurate and realistic when you answer the questions they will put to you. Cheating on your input would be like cheating at solitaire. What's the point?

A major advantage of the digital approach to retirement planning is the ease with which you can revise the plan. The program does all the math for you (and never makes a mistake); all you have to do is enter any significant changes in your circumstances or your assumptions about the future. This makes it a cinch to keep your plan realistic and up-to-date.

***

If you don't want to spend the twenty bucks or so that a retirement program will cost you, just log on to the Internet. There are literally hundreds of Web sites that provide retirement planning guidance for no charge at all. Some of them are quite good. Of course, they don't provide the convenience and attention to detail that you'll get from a standalone package; still, for the price, what can you lose?

Here is a tiny sampling of some of the better sites:

- www.asec.org
- www.financenter.com
- www.financialengines.com
- www.mfea.com
- www.quicken.com

Try one or more of them. You're sure to find one that pleases.

***

Perhaps the best way of all to determine whether you're on track on your retirement planning is the preparation of a net worth report once a year. A net worth report in its simplest form is a listing of all your assets minus all of your liabilities.

It's easy to determine your net worth at any point in time. First, add up the value of everything you own. For non-cash items, the value will be what you could reasonably expect to sell the item for. The total of all these items, investments, bank accounts, cars, real estate, jewelry—everything with a value—equals your assets. Then add up everything you owe. These are your liabilities. Subtract your liabilities from your assets and what is left over is your net worth.

You don't have to know the exact value of everything to calculate your assets. A reasonable estimate for those items that don't have a specific market value will do just fine. Some financial purists suggest that you should not include items such as cars and jewelry in your list of assets because you aren't likely to sell them. In my view, that's an academic point that is of little consequence. If it makes you feel warm and fuzzy to include them, go ahead. I've done so for many years. So long as you are consistent in what you do or do not include, your annual net worth report will tell you what you want to know: Am I increasing my net worth each year? Am I managing my debts well? How are my investments doing?

Once you get into the habit of preparing an annual net worth statement, you'll never want to stop. If you'll forgive a strained metaphor, your preparation for a secure retirement is a journey down a long road. You don't want to set out on that kind of trip without some way to measure how far you've traveled and whether you're on schedule. An annual net worth statement will bring you face-to-face with the facts.

CHAPTER THIRTEEN
Keeping Your Golden Years Golden

Fear no more the heat o' th' sun,
Nor the furious winter's rages.
Thou thy worldly task hast done,
Home art gone and ta'en thy wages.
—William Shakespeare (1564–1616)

O.K., so you've done all the right things—as good as or better than you've read in these pages. No more spreadsheets, calculations, or charts telling you how much money you'll need to fund a comfortable retirement. It's too late for that now, even if any of those gadgets could really calculate such an infinitely variable unknown. Retirement time has finally arrived. What you've got now is what you've got.

But that's fine. You've built up a hefty kitty that should keep you in beer and pretzels, allow for two weeks in Miami every February, and still leave a little for the kids.

Or will it? How can you make sure that your nice nest egg won't crack?

Answering that question would be easy if you knew exactly how long you're going to live, though I can't imagine why anyone would want to know that. Personally, I prefer to keep it a surprise.

An old friend of mine had a favorite little routine he would play out whenever the subject of mortality and money came up. "I have enough money to last me the rest of my life," he would say, glancing intently at his watch, "provided I go at..."

But seriously, how long are YOU going to live?

You can't answer that question, of course, unless you're planning to do away with yourself in the next few minutes. Since you've read this far, I'll chalk that up as unlikely. All the more reason for you to know that scientists who estimate future life spans are coming up with some interesting generalities. "A 70-year-old today is like a 60-year-old 10 years ago," says Ronald Klatz, president of the American Academy of Anti-Aging Medicine. "Within the next 35 years, people are going to be turning 100 and feeling like they are at 55 today."

In short, regardless of your age, scientists are saying that you're likely to live longer than you may think. Forget about your parents and grandparents and their ages when they died. Comparisons with their life spans and yours are becoming less and less relevant. Extraordinary progress in health care as well as healthier diets and a better awareness of fitness have combined to extend average life spans at an unprecedented rate.

Another major factor in your financial future is your present age. Did you work until you were 70 years of age? Or did you take that golden parachute at age 55? Obviously, a half-million or so in the bank would probably stand you in good stead in the former case, but may well expire before the latter.

So how long will your retirement fund last? Will it still be around if you live another 10, 20, 30 years or longer? Take a look at Figure 3. This chart tells you how long your money will last at various rates of return, assuming a modest 3% inflation rate.

%of capital withdrawn in 1ˢᵗ year	4% return	5% return	6% return	7% return	8% return	9% return	10% return	11% return	12% return	13% return	14% return
ASSUMING 3% INFLATION Your money will last this many years, if your original withdrawal rises by 3% annually and your money is invested at the following average rates of return											
2%	68	158	#	#	#	#	#	#	#	#	#
3%	40	52	100	#	#	#	#	#	#	#	#
4%	28	34	43	72	#	#	#	#	#	#	#
5%	22	25	29	36	55	#	#	#	#	#	#
6%	18	20	22	26	31	44	#	#	#	#	#
7%	15	17	18	20	23	27	36	#	#	#	#
8%	13	14	15	17	18	21	24	31	#	#	#
9%	12	12	13	14	15	17	19	22	27	44	#
10%	10	11	12	12	13	14	15	17	19	23	33
11%	9	10	10	11	12	12	13	14	16	18	21
12%	9	9	9	10	10	11	11	12	13	14	16
13%	8	8	9	9	9	10	10	11	11	12	13
!4%	7	8	8	8	8	9	9	10	10	11	12
15%	7	7	7	8	8	8	8	9	9	10	10

Figure 4
Assumes a single withdrawal at the start of each year.
All numbers are rounded.
Source: John Allen of Allen-Warren, Arvada, CO

To show you how the chart works, let's assume that you expect to get an 8% return on your investment portfolio and that you will withdraw 10% in the first year. Since we are assuming a 3% inflation rate, you will increase your withdrawal by 3% each year in order to maintain the same purchasing power. Follow the 10% withdrawal row over to the 8% rate of return. There you see that your money will last 13 years. Not bad if you're 80 years old; not so good if you're a sprightly 55.

Remember, this chart assumes a relatively modest 3% inflation rate. Increase inflation and your money's longevity decreases proportionately.

So what can you do if it appears that your money is going to run out before you do? You can look around for ways to lower your expenses, or you can set out to develop a higher return on your investments. And don't rule out a part-time job. That can be a lot of fun and can brighten up your financial picture considerably.

The bottom line: You may have what looks like lots of bucks put aside for your bonus years, but you simply can't afford to let up on the principles of sound money management if you want to ensure a snug retirement.

If you're sneaking at peak at this chapter before you qualify for retirement, shame on you. All the same, congratulate yourself for learning just how important it is to employ the principles of sound money management as early as possible.

***

Perhaps the most often-heard advice to people beginning their retirement years is the sober admonition to "preserve your principal."

I want to point out to you again that **protecting your purchasing power should be your objective in retirement**, not preserving your principal. In fact, setting out to "preserve your principal" is a sure road to a steady reduction in your purchasing power. Inflation is the bad guy.

Let's take the case of fictional Joe Gullible. Joe has heard all his life about the need to preserve his principal. "Live off the interest," he was advised when he retired, "but whatever you do, don't touch the principal."

Taking this advice to heart, Joe concentrated solely on investing his $300,000 life savings into instruments guaranteed to preserve his principle. And it worked. He lived off his Social Security, his pension, and all of the interest from his savings. After 10 years of retirement Joe still had his $300,000 in principal.

But here's the rub: Because of Demon Inflation, the purchasing power of that stash was now worth a little more than three-quarters of what it was worth when he started. If Joe lives another 10 years in the same fashion, the purchasing power of his savings will have shrunk to less than half of its original value. And that's going on the rosy and probably unwise assumption that inflation will not rise any higher than the relatively modest rate of recent years.

That's the evil of inflation. It causes a loss of principal without appearing to cause a loss of principal. Even Stephen King couldn't come up with a more diabolic villain than Demon Inflation.

And that's why the principles in this book are every bit as important in retirement as they are during your working life. Increasing your assets at a greater rate than the rate of inflation is the only way to ensure a financially comfortable retirement, not to mention the preservation of whatever you want to leave to your heirs.

So, our final principle of sound financial management is:

- **Design your retirement financial plan to provide growth without undue risk.**

To be sure, your approach to investment can and should be modified once that big direct deposit salary check is no longer being credited to your account every two weeks. When your high earning years are over, it won't be so easy to replace money lost to a fast-talking bond salesman or an adventurous fling with the vagaries of Wall Street.

Even a little financial imprudence on the part of retirees can exact a heavy toll. In the worst case scenario, all can be lost. Bankruptcies by senior citizens are rising sharply all over America. One bankruptcy attorney has said that about one in ten bankruptcies he sees involves senior citizens.

But not to worry. Here's something that may surprise you. Many people have found ways to live higher on the hog in retirement than they did during their so-called bread-winning years. I know a number of people who have done exactly that, and I think you can too. But you'll have to pay attention.

Let's take a quick look at the financial advantages that retirement brings from the first day. Whether you were an executive who had to spring for a couple of new Brooks Brothers suits and a pair of Allan Edmond's shoes every year, or a waiter who had to furnish his own work clothes, your clothing budget will shrink dramatically. Not to suggest that you won't want to stay in style while you're schlepping about town, but the demands on your pocketbook will ease considerably as you learn to drape yourself in *Tres chic* casual.

And don't forget those lunches five days a week, transportation to and from work, and the weekly football pool that you never won. I'll assume, too, that you wouldn't be retiring if your mortgage hadn't already been laid quietly to rest.

No doubt you can come with a few other working-days expenses to toss into the calculations as you tote up the dollar value of the windfall you're about to enjoy.

But wait. Since these expenses are work-related and since you won't be going off to work every day, you won't need that money to maintain your current lifestyle.

Now you're getting the idea. Let's say that you've calculated that your reduction in expenses will amount to $1,000 per month (but it doesn't matter if it's a more modest $500 or even $300). Since you won't need this money to maintain your lifestyle, You're going to invest it every month in your reduced risk portfolio. Not only are you going to beat Demon Inflation, you're going to get a jump on him.

As each year passes, your portfolio, and thus your income, is going to grow at a rate higher than inflation. Even while maintaining your prudent and conservative approach to managing your money, you're going to maintain and even improve your lifestyle. All this while those poor unenlightened souls who blew their work-related reduction in expenses are sweating out their dwindling resources.

This would be good time to go back and review the principles of sound money management in chapters three, four and five. The basic principles don't change in retirement, the only thing that changes is your vulnerability to risk. A temporary downturn in the market may not be temporary enough given your present circumstances.

**

But don't let your new sensitivity to risk get the upper hand. If your local insurance agent gets wind of that pile of cash you're sitting on he may pitch a special instrument called an immediate fixed annuity. It works like this: You give the company a big hunk of money and they guarantee you a monthly check for a fixed amount for the rest of your life. The size of the check will depend on complex calculations based on the amount of your payment, your age, your sex, prevailing interest rates and a bunch of esoteric stuff that they probably won't tell you.

On the surface, fixed annuities look like attractive investments for retirees. In fact, for the totally chicken-hearted, they may be acceptable, especially when the retirement nest egg is tiny with no margin for loss. Once you buy your annuity, that monthly payment will come in for the rest of your life, no matter how long you live (be sure to pick a healthy company). A fixed annuity is one sure way to shift the worry about managing your portfolio to someone else.

But I don't like annuities. Here's why:

#1. The amount of your payment will never change. The longer you live, the less it will buy (Remember Demon Inflation).

#2. With most types of annuities, there won't be anything left over for the kids when you die. Maybe that's OK with you, but don't forget #1.

The best way to modify your portfolio to reduce the element of risk without giving up the battle against Demon Inflation is to adjust your asset allocation of stocks and bonds. Let's say that you maintained an average mix of 65% equities (stocks), 25% bonds, and 10% cash during your wild oats years (not a bad recipe). Now that your metabolism has eased up a notch or two, you may want to dampen the financial hearth to keep it in tune with your changing circumstances.

Adjusting to 30% equities, 50% bonds and 20% cash equivalents (CDs, money markets, etc.) should provide you with the peace of mind that comes with minimal risk while keeping a toe in the capital growth waters.

More than ever, you must concentrate on high quality securities. The equities portion of your portfolio should consist entirely of mutual funds. This is no time to be dabbling in individual stocks. Several index funds, each one pegged to a different market index may be all the decision-making you'll need to keep Demon Inflation (and the wolf) away from your door.

The same with bonds. Stick to the wide variety of bond funds available instead of trying to pick and choose from the mind-boggling assortment of individual bonds that only the professionals can size up with any degree of accuracy.

You or your advisors may prefer a slightly different asset allocation than the one mentioned above. That's fine. What matters is that you avoid the mistake of Joe Gullible. The only way to protect your purchasing power during retirement is to maintain a reasonable percentage of your portfolio invested in equities that promise that all-important inflation-busting growth.

***

Fortunately, your investment portfolio doesn't have to carry the entire load. One of the bonuses that comes with retirement are those neat little ways to stretch your retirement dollars that will be popping up all around you. The so-called senior discount is one of the neatest and perhaps one of the most underused of the retirement perks.

From the tiny discounts at McDonald's and Burger King to those tidy discounts on movie and theater tickets, to the big bucks to be saved on travel and lodging, the senior discount is serendipity at its best. I'll have to admit that some sort of misplaced vanity kept me from claiming my largesse when I first stepped into the qualifying arena. I suspect that most new senior citizens (I hate that label, but I can't come up with a better one) are reluctant to publicly proclaim their new status by asking for a senior discount.

My spouse was my inspiration in the senior discount derby. Never shy from the first day she qualified, Betty was happy to announce her fiscal triumphs each time she saved a buck or two (or 25 cents) simply by asking for the discount. Still I demurred.

After holding out valiantly for a respectable time, I finally gave in to my wife's irrefutable logic. The senior discount was found money. I still remember the first time I dipped a toe in the discount waters. As I inched my way toward the cashier's cage at the local multiplex I was hoping against hope that the cashier would respond to my request for a senior's discount by saying, "I'm sorry, sir, I'll have to see your ID." (She didn't.) Still, the four bucks I saved on the tickets raised my enjoyment level of the movie immensely. (No one has yet demanded I show my ID before allowing my discount, but hope springs eternal.)

How many after-tax dollars you can save by judicious claiming of the senior discount will depend on such things as your persistence level and how active you are. In our case, I estimate that we probably save about $200 or $300 per year. Not a lot of money, of course, but enough to spring for a couple of dinners, a copy of the latest New York Times best-seller and a bottle of good wine.

Claiming your share of senior discounts isn't going to elevate your lifestyle, but once you get over the fear of asking, you're going to be surprised at how frequently the opportunity to save an after-tax dollar or two presents itself.

Keeping the tax man at bay is no less important after retirement than it is during your peak earning years, perhaps more important. With less money coming in, you need to do everything possible to keep your tax drain to a minimum.

One opportunity to do that is when you find it necessary to tap your portfolio for a little cash. Whenever it's necessary to liquidate any of your holdings, be sure to pick assets that will trigger the least tax when you sell them. First, look for assets that show the least capital gains. If you're selling a portion of one stock, be sure to sell the shares purchased at the highest price. You should also look for stocks that you have held for at least one year so that you'll pay the long-term capital gains tax rate of 20% rather than your marginal tax rate.

As a rule, avoid selling any part of your tax-deferred investments such as IRA and 401(k) retirement accounts. These instruments are among the best tools you have for fending off the tax man. Of course, you'll have to pay taxes on these funds when you begin mandatory withdrawals at age 70 1/2. Before then, however, they are the last place you should look for spending money.

***

Building a nest egg adequate to provide for a worry-free retirement is a smart move. Still, important though it may be, money isn't enough to guarantee contentment in your final years. It would be logical to assume that a leisurely life free of financial pressures would be all one needs to fill the golden years with happiness.

But it's not that simple.

Over the years, I've had ample opportunity to observe what I've come to call the irrelevant senior. Let me explain.

While your career is in full swing, no matter what your calling, your life is a nonstop merry-go-round of social and business relationships. It's something we don't notice because it's been with us forever. We talk with people, we argue with them, we exchange philosophies. We come into contact with a variety of business associates every day. We meet people who want our opinions, or at least want us to listen to theirs. More important, we forge relationships at the workplace. Relationships that we assume are friendships destined to live forever. In short, we are relevant. We matter. We are a part of the exciting world around us.

For more people than you might imagine, that relevancy ends with retirement. The first trip or two back to the office or the plant after the presentation of the gold watch is met with enthusiasm and camaraderie. Old friends are happy to see us. Work stops while nostalgia runs its course. It usually goes downhill from there.

One or two more visits and the retiree senses that she's "in the way," even if she used to run the place—**especially** if she used to run the place. The new boss may frown at what he feels is an intrusion affecting productivity. Visits to the workplace are over.

At home. It's all too easy fall into the mind-numbing routine of mowing the lawn, fixing the plumbing and watching the late show. Our circle of friends narrows and the cycle of boredom picks up speed. Irrelevancy sets in.

I've seen far too many men and women sink into destructive irrelevancy in their later years. They may not describe their situation with that word, of course, may not even be aware of their plight. Still, they know at the deepest level that their opinions are no longer sought; they are genuinely needed by fewer and fewer people; they go largely unnoticed at gatherings where they might once have been the star attraction

Irrelevancy doesn't happen only to carpenters, dentists, and computer technicians. It can and does happen to corporate presidents and movie stars. Irrelevancy respects no boundaries. Once it sets in, irrelevancy chips away at self-esteem, ambition, and self-confidence. Serious depression often results from neglected irrelevancy.

Fortunately, irrelevancy is easy to vanquish. But it must be stopped in its tracks before it gets a hold on you.

During your working years, most of your efforts were aimed at satisfying a myriad of responsibilities to yourself and your family. A self-centered interest, one might say. And rightfully so. In our society, we are taught that work is a means to the good life. Taking good care of our families (and ourselves) is at the top of our list of priorities.

For most people, retirement comes after most or all of those responsibilities have been reasonably fulfilled. Sometimes that situation leaves an invisible but persistent vacuum. Filling that vacuum is the key to banishing irrelevancy and continuing a productive and satisfying life until it's time to shuffle off this mortal coil.

There are almost as many ways to fill that vacuum and banish irrelevancy as there are people. In general, post- retirement activities fall into three broad categories: volunteer work, politics/community service, and second-career/part-time work.

For some folks, relevancy needs can be fully satisfied simply by performing volunteer work at local hospitals, charities, libraries and the like. Regardless of your personality, the time available, and your physical circumstances, there is a volunteer job ideally suited to you. Your local hospital almost certainly has a volunteer program. Whether you are best suited to office work or direct patient contact, the hospital almost certainly has a volunteer job that you would enjoy. The same goes for your church or synagogue, local charities and advocacy groups.

If you are a retired businessperson, contact the nearest chapter of the Service Corps of Retired Executives (SCORE). This national organization of retired business executives provides free counseling service to small business owners.

Regardless of your particular area of business expertise, SCORE will provide you with an opportunity to share your knowledge with those who will both appreciate and benefit from your counsel. Irrelevancy can't get a foothold in the life of someone who makes a genuine effort to help others in need.

***

If volunteerism isn't your cup of tea. If you feel the need for a more challenging environment, with perhaps a touch of competition and other adrenalin-pumping qualities, you have a wide choice of ways to keep the irrelevancy monster at bay.

Many people, perhaps you were one of them, spend most of their lives complaining about such things as local and federal governments, politicians, operation of the local municipality or school district, and most other public and municipal concerns—without ever making the slightest attempt to do anything about the problems. **Complaining**, of course, is far safer and easier than **doing**.

Feeling any guilt pangs? If so, now is a good time to make amends. Since you're no longer toiling away in a job or career that takes "all of your time," getting involved in municipal or political affairs is the logical way for you to fill that retirement vacuum.

If you're a registered voter, no matter your political affiliation, there is probably a local organization that would welcome your inquiry about membership. Take it from me, they'll extend a warm welcome and offer a wide variety of ways for you to make up for all those years of non-involvement. If you're not a registered voter, shame on you. Now is the time to take care of that little oversight. As a voter, you automatically become relevant to the efficient functioning of our democratic system.

***

Finally, if none of the above rings any bells for you, you may be a good candidate for a second career. From clerking behind the tobacco counter of your local pharmacy to starting a part-time business from your home, to launching a full-fledged business operation, a second career is a guaranteed immunization against irrelevancy disease.

By its very nature, the demands of any activity in the business arena will involve you directly with living, breathing people. Interaction with a variety of other human beings is the very essence of relevancy in our society. It's also the best defense available against the human tendency to allow our thoughts to focus exclusively on our own problems—a guaranteed way to make those problems seem larger than life.

So there you have it. A financially comfortable life and an effective defense against the irrelevancy monster. What more could you ask for?

Index

4

A

B

C

D

T

U

V

W

Z